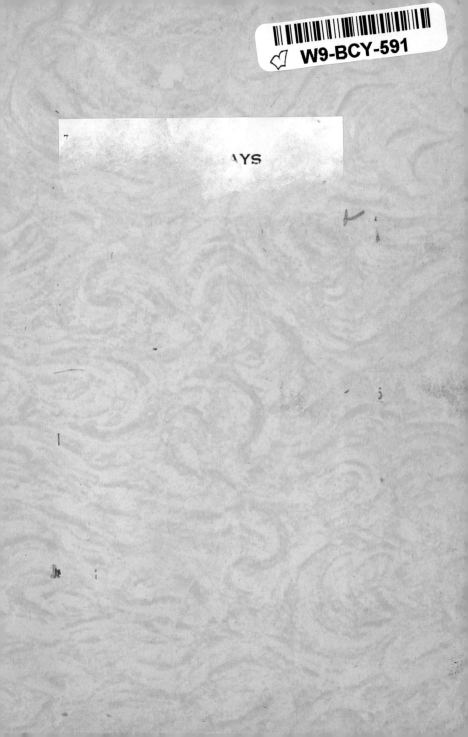

AYS

Music for Fun

Music for Fun

By SIGMUND SPAETH

New York WHITTLESEY HOUSE London
MCGRAW-HILL BOOK COMPANY, INC.

Copyright, 1939, *by* SIGMUND SPAETH

PUBLISHED BY WHITTLESEY HOUSE
A division of the McGraw-Hill Book Company, Inc.

Printed in the United States of America by The Maple Press Co., York, Pa.

TO

*My friends and pupils in Hawaii,
who contributed so much to the
making of this book and have so
thoroughly lived up to its title*

Preface

ONE trouble with music is that the people who know the most about it generally get very little fun out of it. On the other hand, those who honestly enjoy music, but admit they know nothing about it, often have their pleasure spoiled by an inferiority complex which is assiduously fed by those superior beings who, by training or talent or both, have achieved the rank of "artist" or "critic" or "scholar."

Plenty of books have been written for the ones who already know quite a lot about music, and perhaps too many for those who know something but are willing to be taught more. Comparatively little has been written for those who are frankly ignorant of the whole subject. They have been encouraged to say "It's all over my head" or, at best, "I don't know anything about music but I know what I like." They have been led to believe that the entire art is shrouded in mystery, which only the elect can penetrate, and that they will be satisfied with dumb reverence if they know their place.

The old-fashioned teacher started with the thesis that music was hard work, which it unquestionably had been for him. It was presented to the pupil as a duty and a drudgery. The idea that anybody could have quite a lot of fun with music without particularly working at it never seemed to occur to anyone. Even today that suggestion horrifies most of the highbrows. It is just beginning to be realized that music might occasionally be worth pursuing merely for pleasure, without any thought of impressing other people by one's performance or scholarship, and certainly without any intention of making a living out of it.

Let there be no misunderstanding as to this writer's attitude in the matter. He admits that to become a professional musician, or even a good amateur, is a difficult task, requiring the hardest kind of work, plus a certain amount of talent. But he also believes that there are millions of people who could have fun with music, just as they have fun with eating, drinking, sleeping, and breathing, without the slightest technical knowledge of the subject.

This book is written for those millions, and the less they know about music the better. It assumes merely that a majority of people respond to some kind of music with pleasure, and that they might enjoy expressing this pleasure more definitely and consciously, though not a bit less sincerely, than they now do. It accepts the fact that multitudes of honest music-lovers are by nature incapable of the sort of performance that would satisfy even themselves, not to mention the neighbors; but it nevertheless insists that some participation in music is possible for far more people than perhaps realize it at present, so long as their standards are not too high.

The underlying thought is always, "If you yourself are enjoying music, either as a participant or as a listener, that is all that matters. You do not have to inflict your performance or your tastes on anyone else. Nor do you have to go through a lot of dull drudgery in order to show off your skill to people who might not appreciate it after all. So long as you are having a good time expressing yourself musically, don't worry about the effect on others. They don't have to listen."

This book merely tries to stimulate such a normal enthusiasm for music. It suggests ways of getting started, for adults and children alike, with practical hints to parents on catching their children early, and suggestions to those who missed the encouragement they should have had in their own childhood. In no sense does it attempt to teach music to anybody. It has a few things to say about how anyone can start in to become an appreciative listener as well as a self-raising performer. But for the latter it frankly urges an early contact with a good, progressive teacher, if the preliminary fun has encouraged any thought of more serious application; and for the outright listener it recommends a wide variety of aids that could not possibly be included in this book.

Preface

If music is to be treated as fun, there is an excuse for lightness of approach, even an occasional bit of clowning. Those who take themselves and their music very seriously are assured that no irreverence is intended either to the art itself or to its established disciples. In such a book the accent must be on the fun rather than on the music, and if anyone is insulted, let's admit that what we are talking about isn't really music at all. But it is a most interesting and exciting phase of human nature, whose potential appeal is too widespread and significant to be ignored.

SIGMUND SPAETH.

Contents

Contents

[xii]

Contents

Music for Fun

INTRODUCTORY

At a liberal estimate, perhaps 1 per cent of the entire population of the United States may be considered honestly interested in good music. This includes all the musical performers, amateur as well as professional, and all those who can fairly be called music-lovers. It does not include the jitterbugs or those who merely dance to the latest tune.

Comparatively few of America's 1,300,000 musicians and music-lovers really get fun out of music. Take, first of all, the admittedly great artists, of whom there are never more than about fifty in circulation at one time. Most of them do not enjoy their music at all, although they probably did in the earlier stages of their careers. They have become slaves to music, sacrifices to a public whose demands upon them are unjust and implacable. They are not permitted to live normal lives, but must travel constantly and dwell in perpetual relation to a potential or actual audience. They cannot do as they please, eat and drink what they wish, see their friends informally, arrange their time to suit themselves.

[3]

Music is their taskmaster. They spend hours in practice
even after reaching the heights. They watch their
figures, guard against unfavorable publicity, autograph
pictures and programs interminably. Any false step may
be fatal. They are surrounded by managers, press agents,
salesmen, income tax collectors, benefit chairmen. They
live in constant terror of a bad performance or a cold
audience. They make lots of money, but have little
chance to spend it. Adulation has become a bore, and the
most popular pieces in their repertoire are a nightmare
of deadly familiarity. The great artists do not get much
fun out of music.

Then there are the artists who may be called good, but
not necessarily great. They have all the problems of the
big stars, but fewer of the rewards. Their sacrifices are
just as great, and their prohibitions just as constant.
They work even harder than the established virtuosi
and have perhaps less fun on the whole. Very little of
their enjoyment of life comes from music itself.

ARTISTS AND TRADESMEN

The struggling artists, on the border line between the
professional and the top-notch amateur, have the worst
time of all. Often they do not make an adequate living,
but try to keep up appearances so that the public will
not know that they are hopelessly in debt, perhaps close
to starvation. They cannot assume the grand manner
without sufficient reason, and if they act like human
beings they are accused of having no temperament. They

are continually torn by doubts as to whether they should not be making a living as clerks or stenographers or insurance salesmen, and many of them actually do some such thing to keep alive, and practice their music on the side. They are harassed by constant demands upon their talents, without financial return, and torn between the desire for publicity and the economic necessity of putting a price on their performances. Often they have to be their own promoters, press agents, managers, and secretaries. They do not have the time or the spiritual freedom to get much fun out of music itself.

Next come the tradesmen of music. They are the drudges, the hack workers, the clock punchers, the salaried working class, to whom music is no more fun than baseball is to the average professional. They are generally disappointed artists who gave up the hopeless task of achieving individual recognition and are now in the throes of cut-throat competition with their fellow laborers. Music has become a fearful grind for them, although some of them still enjoy a busman's holiday occasionally, when they play what and as they please. They all belong to the Musicians' Union, which numbers about 130,000 in the whole country, with 19,000 in New York's Local 802 alone. The Union does not recognize singers as musicians. You have to be an instrumentalist to qualify. You are also forbidden to accept less than a minimum wage for your work, even though you may be out of a job for months at a time. You are weighed down with rules and regulations and restrictions, and not allowed to get much fun out of music, even if you should feel like it, which you generally don't if you are that kind of musician.

Music teachers should be considered as a separate class, although many of them belong also to one of the other professional categories. They likewise are often disappointed performers, and they have most of the unhappiness of the musical tradesmen, with even less recognition or financial return. Teaching itself is drudgery of the worst sort, unless one is an inspired pedagogue, with a love of that art for its own sake and a sympathetic enthusiasm for even the dullest pupil. Many people are teachers because they cannot do anything else, and this is by no means restricted to music. But a good music teacher may easily enjoy both the teaching and the music, especially if occasional opportunities for personal performance are included in his life. There is at least the satisfaction of receiving public appreciation, and the income, though modest, is likely to be steady.

THE ATTITUDE OF THE AMATEUR

In the amateur class of musicians and music-lovers there are, first of all, those who play or sing well enough to be near-professionals, and who consequently are seldom satisfied to remain the amateurs that they should be. On the whole, however, they enjoy music, and this is even more true of those who are aware of their limitations and play for their own pleasure rather than to show off or make a little money on the side. There are a few amateurs, scattered throughout the country, who get fun out of meeting in groups, playing together, and exchanging musical ideas, and this includes some of the so-called music clubs. There is also a fairly large group of amateur and semiprofessional singers who honestly enjoy music, usually by way of church choirs, glee clubs, and choral societies. Their pleasure is partly social, but also significantly musical, and there ought to be more of them.

NONPARTICIPANTS AND HANGERS-ON

Finally there is a considerable number of sincere music-lovers who do not participate in music at all, but go regularly to concerts when they have the opportunity, buy good phonograph records, and tune in on the best radio programs. They even read books on music, which entitles them to some special credit. These nonparticipating music-lovers are supplemented by a few hypocrites, culture hounds, gushers, faddists, and social idlers, but even with these additions the class is not large. It practically never suffices to support a vigorous musical program in any community.

All these classes of musicians and music-lovers, taken together, do not total more than 1 per cent of the American population. Of the remaining 99 per cent, more people today can get and are getting fun out of music than is possible for most of the self-confessed amateurs and professionals. This book is addressed to the 128,700,-000 potential music-lovers rather than the 1,300,000 who have already arrived, although there is no objection to having anyone in this smaller group read it.

The potential music-lovers have been kept out of the sacred circle chiefly because music was represented to them as a complete mystery, or possibly as a difficult task, an unpleasant duty, or an endless drudgery. For the professional musician, or even the well-trained amateur, it may be all of those things. But for the person who is not worrying about either making a living out of music or showing off to friends, music should be pure fun, a constant pleasure, and an ideal recreation. The one whose ideals of performance or intellectual appreciation are not too high is likely to get the most fun out of music. I have never seen anyone who could not enjoy a good meal, but very few of those people knew anything about cooking; and to be able to cook, or to discuss the intricacies of the art with the technique of a gourmet, would not have added appreciably to their enjoyment of food. Similarly, I can think of practically no one, excepting Dr. Samuel Johnson, with a positive distaste for music, and the enjoyment of it has seldom shown any great dependence on a technical understanding or intensive training.

JITTERBUGS AND THE SWING CRAZE

The jitterbugs who crowd around the kings of swing, as they lead their bands, all over the country, are getting fun out of music, although they know little or nothing about it, and could not analyze their emotions in any case. They do not realize that their response to hot jazz is a combination of the physical reflex action induced by a powerful and persistent rhythm and the thoroughly human reaction to extraordinary skill of any kind. Swing is nothing but improvised variations on a popular tune, and these variations have come to follow a fairly constant set of patterns, with rather monotonous results. But the technique of the players is amazing, placing them far in advance of the performers who were doing exactly the same thing, with less skill, twenty years ago.

CLASSIC PARALLELS

Just as the serious musicians, scholars, critics, artists, and teachers have always built up and maintained a veil of mystery around music as a whole, so the disciples and high priests of swing have encouraged a similar attitude, leading to the utterance of an incredible amount of nonsense, both spoken and written. Yet on the whole, the lovers of swing (most of whom are at least sincere) have a better time with music than the fanatics of symphony and opera. What they do not realize is that they could have an equally good time with music of a higher quality. Their reactions to rhythm, melody, harmony, and tone color could be stimulated just as effectively by compositions of some permanent value, for the ingredients are essentially the same. The technique of a Heifetz could astonish them as much as that of a Benny Goodman. The scholarly variations of a Brahms on a theme perhaps more significant than *Sweet Sue* could eventually produce as much surprise and pleasure as the supposedly extempore but actually routine decorations of a conventional tune by Count Basie or Lionel Hampton.

If you are going to get fun out of music, the first necessity is to dismiss all thoughts of duty or self-consciousness and be completely honest. That is the great advantage enjoyed by the jitterbugs at the moment. They may not be able to keep time, but at least they move their feet sincerely. Popular music in general has enjoyed a consistently truthful response that the so-called "classics" could rarely claim. That is why popular composers make a living, which the serious ones almost never do.

Did it ever occur to you that anyone at all should be able to play some musical instrument, at least for his or her own pleasure, to sing agreeably, also primarily for personal satisfaction, and to read and write notes as easily as one reads and writes one's own language?

MUSIC AND LANGUAGE

The only reason why this is not a general condition is that music is not taught as the language that it should be considered. We learn our own tongue first by ear. Later we go to school and find out how to read, write, and spell the language with which we are already quite familiar.

Parents would not dream of sending their children to school without a fairly large working vocabulary and the ability to understand their own language, at least in its simpler forms. School-teachers are practically never asked to educate a completely inarticulate, totally illiterate child. Yet this is what music teachers are constantly asked to do. They are given pupils who have never become acquainted with the most obvious fundamentals of even rhythm and melody, and are expected to teach these little morons how to read, write, and express vocally and instrumentally a language that is a complete mystery to them.

DID THIS HAPPEN TO YOU?

The unmusical adults of today are probably aware of this, although they may never have stopped to analyze the situation. Most of you who are now looking back regretfully on your lack of musical experience probably had your share of "music lessons" of the old-fashioned type. You had had little or no parental guidance or encouragement before you were thrown to a music teacher, and you were never told that all these things about notes and tones, and melodies, rhythms and harmonies, might be just a lot of fun and not hard work at all.

Modern parents have doubtless improved, as have the teachers, but there are still far too many homes where the parents have never bothered to develop any real enthusiasm for music either in their offspring or in themselves. With all the up-to-date musical resources and equipment at their command, they have failed to utilize the formative years of preschool age to find out what their children could do musically or to lay a permanent foundation for the future enjoyment of music by the entire family.

OUT OF THE MOUTHS OF BABES

Let the musically neglected child speak for itself: "Listen, Momma. From the day I was born you had a chance to let me hear music. There was a phonograph in the house, and a radio, and even a piano, although no one ever played on it. Did I ever hear any of them? No. What I heard was baby talk, all day and half the night. I would never have learned to pronounce my own language properly if I hadn't picked things up in the street. For a long time I thought there wasn't any tense but the past. I got awfully sick of being told, 'He was a lovely baby, yes, he *was*.' Half the time I didn't even hear those final s's, they were so often pronounced as d's. 'Yed, he wud.' What kind of English is that, anyway?

"But at least by the time I got to be six going on seven and went to school, I had some idea of what people were talking about. I had heard an awful lot of bad English by that time, but I could understand and talk it in a fashion. When my teacher taught me how to spell 'cat,' I didn't have to be told what a cat was, or what it looked like. I had seen our cat and pulled its tail, and the sound of cat meant cat to me and nothing else. I'm a pretty good speller already.

[12]

"But what did you do about music? Nothing, Momma. I heard practically no music on the phonograph or the radio that sounded nice to me. When I tried to play on the piano, at an early age, I was told to stop that noise. Did you yourself ever try to sing to me? Not unless my ears deceived me. There's no excuse in saying you aren't musical and never were. Would I have known the difference? And did it ever occur to you that you might have learned how to carry a tune yourself, and maybe even to play it on the piano, while I was too young to check up on you? In my childish innocence I thought everything you did was pretty swell. I probably could have stood even your interpretation of music. Then by the time I was old enough to know better, you might have improved enough to satisfy my more critical ear. We might even have learned our little pieces together and turned practice into a perpetual game. (Did you hear that word 'perpetual'?)

THAT'S TELLING 'EM, KID

"You can't say you didn't have *time* to develop my musical instincts. Think of how much time you wasted, not only with baby talk, but in shaking rattles in front of my face, squeezing silly little rubber things, building something out of blocks, cutting something out of paper, putting dolls through all sorts of contortions. I often heard you say, 'I can't think *what* to do next to keep this child occupied.' Wouldn't it have been a joke on you if simply turning on a phonograph record had given me the habit of keeping quiet? You never made any effort to find out.

"When I started to bang on the keyboard of the piano, the way every kid I know does at some time or other, you didn't have sense enough to discover if I might be interested in turning the noise into a tune or a harmony. I've heard of musical geniuses who started just that way. They found out that it sounded better if tones made sense, played one after another, or all at once in a chord. Somebody helped them pick out the first few patterns, and then they went ahead and discovered the rest for themselves.

ARE TESTS NECESSARY?

"All these years, from the time I was a day old until my present advanced age of nearly seven, were completely wasted so far as music was concerned. I've heard of babies that kept time to music before they could walk. You never found out if I could do it, because there wasn't any music to keep time to. I'm told that plenty of kids have been able to hum a tune before they could talk. But if I never heard a tune, how could I hum anything?

"Now some old professor wants to test me with a record to find out if I ought to take music lessons. He wants to try my sense of time and pitch and my feeling for harmony. If you had been finding out all that through musical games, these past years, I wouldn't *have* to be tested now. Maybe I wouldn't be a musician, but at least I would know music the way I know my own language. I probably wouldn't hate the idea of music lessons the way I do. Altogether, I think we both ought to be sorry we didn't make music a part of our lives right from the start."

SO HERE IS THE ANSWER

Why not admit that this imaginary child is absolutely right? Many of us have had exactly the same feeling, although we never expressed it so forcibly. At least we are aware today that something was lacking in our earliest years that might have made a big difference later.

Something can still be done about it, even by the grown-ups. Music need not be a closed book to you just because you failed to get the proper start as a child. You have made many discoveries in your adult years, and you can just as easily add a few on the subject of music.

If you have children of your own, you can avoid the mistakes that were made in your case and can develop your enjoyment of music as the children are developing theirs. But the suggestions contained in the following pages are by no means limited to parents and children. Anybody at all can apply them in a practical fashion, and it is never too late to start. The extent to which they are followed will depend on the individual, with due regard for differences in taste, enthusiasm, intelligence, financial circumstances, and leisure time.

Be assured that these suggestions have all been put to practical tests. They work. No one of average mentality, young or old, has ever failed to respond to these simple and obvious methods of approaching music as a recreation. There is no mystery about it, no elaborate formula, no endless discussion of psychology.

You can try these little tricks or experiments, or whatever you wish to call them, on your piano or phonograph or some other musical instrument, or work them out with the cooperation of the local music store, or even to some extent with voices alone. You can form a group or a club and in that way share both a common enthusiasm and a common equipment. The ways and means can be found if the spirit is willing and the flesh equal to some slight exertion. At no time need music make any physical or mental demands upon you beyond those of golf, bridge, ping-pong, or backgammon. If you have any hobbies at all, why not make music one of them?

PRELIMINARIES TO PARTICIPATION

Just as you have to hear a language before you can speak it, so you should hear some music before you try to make any. A child can listen to music of some sort for at least two or three years before attempting to take part in it. Similarly the adult inclination to participate in music is logically preceded by a fairly extensive hearing of all kinds of pieces.

This may have been automatic and practically unconscious. But even so, a fairly definite line of progress is generally evident. Human beings instinctively follow the line of least resistance. With a baby this means obvious rhythms and melodies, nursery rhymes of the simplest sort, anything that is easily assimilated and easily remembered. With an adult it means popular tunes, jazz, and the "light classics." (Swing could be included, as far as its basic rhythms and melodies are concerned, but its elaborate technique demands more than the mere reflex action created by the average product of Tin-Pan Alley).

[17]

Check up on your musical experience and see how familiar you are with the outstanding melodies of the world, the music that has proved its permanence even though it may be far from "classic" standards. This is the sort of music that should be introduced as early as possible to children, either through phonograph records or, better still, through the parental voice or instrumental performance.

Actually, of course, it would be ridiculous to argue that one piece sounds different from another to a newborn babe. Anything at all will do at the outset, so long as it is music and not mere noise. It is impossible to say just how early a child's ear begins to differentiate sounds, especially such complicated sounds as occur even in a simple piece of music. But since his point of conscious attention is so uncertain, probably varying greatly with different individuals, there is all the more reason for playing safe immediately and always using material that could be considered worth remembering for the future. Certainly there is no harm in selecting a child's musical background from the very start and hoping that some of it may soon become a part of its conscious experience.

RHYTHM IS THE STARTING-POINT

✓ Mankind responds first of all to rhythm, and it is fair to assume that this factor in music will first catch the attention of a child. Strongly marked rhythmic pieces—marches, waltzes, jigs—should convey the earliest audible impressions to the baby whose parents are laying the foundations of a future musical development.

[18]

To be specific, there are plenty of American compositions, available on phonograph records, whose rhythmic spirit will stir both the normal child and its parents. *Turkey in the Straw* is one of the finest of lively tunes, and it has been well arranged by David Guion. *The Arkansas Traveler* is of similar quality, with a story attached to it that may later prove interesting to a boy or a girl.

There is nothing wrong with *Dixie* as a stirring melody, and the same appeal may be found in Foster's *Oh, Susanna* and *Camptown Races*. Henry C. Work wrote a piece of the same type in *Kingdom Coming*, also known as *Year of Jubilo*, of which Jerome Kern once made a splendid arrangement.

The Sousa marches are consistently good, with *The Stars and Stripes Forever* outstanding, and honorable mention for the *Washington Post*, *El Capitan*, and a few others. Schubert's *Marche Militaire*, Elgar's *Pomp and Circumstance*, the Hungarian *Rakoczy March*, and the French *Sambre et Meuse* and *Marche Lorraine* will all set infant feet to kicking rhythmically if given a chance.

There is no necessity for developing a precocious chauvinism with *The Star-Spangled Banner* or *America*, but any child will respond to the rhythmic appeal of *Tramp, tramp, tramp, the boys are marching*, *The Battle Cry of Freedom* (*Rally round the flag, boys*), *America the Beautiful*, and the *Battle Hymn of the Republic*, which, if you prefer, you can present as *John Brown's Body* or *One grass-hopper jumped right over the other grass-hopper's back*.

Malbrough, one of the great rhythmic tunes of all time, is perhaps better known as *He's a jolly good fellow* and

We won't go home until morning. There is no harm in an early acquaintance with the tune generally sung as *Hail, hail, the gang's all here*, which is originally a chorus in Gilbert and Sullivan's opera, *The Pirates of Penzance*.

THE WORDS HELP, TOO

For lively music with fascinating words I recommend the universal *Frog Went a-Courtin'*, which originated in England but is now also a hillbilly classic in America, the Irish *Son of a Gambolier*, the Cornish *There is a tavern in the town*, England's *Billy Boy*, the *Irish Washerwoman*, *Clementine*, *Polly-wolly Doodle*, *Yankee Doodle*, *Shoo Fly*, *Shortnin' Bread*, and the old song of *The Mermaid*.

As instrumental pieces for the very young try *Country Gardens*, *Green Sleeves*, *Shepherd's Hey*, *La Cucaracha*, *The girl I left behind*, *Très Moutarde*, and the *Parade of the Wooden Soldiers*. You don't need words either for *The Wearing of the Green*, *Funiculi Funicula*, or *Avec mes sabots*.

These are all great tunes that everyone should know by heart. The sooner one hears them the better. The proper associations will come later.

Waltz time can also be introduced to the newly born via the phonograph, with Johann Strauss naturally leading the way, although Lehar, Friml, and Victor Herbert will also claim recognition, along with such staples as the *Skater's Waltz*. Early experiments with Schubert, Brahms, and even Chopin waltzes may prove worth while.

Meanwhile, the conscientious parent should be learning to sing all the traditional nursery rhymes to their accepted tunes. *Jack and Jill, Tom, Tom, the Piper's Son, Little Miss Muffet, Mary, Mary, Little Bo-peep*, and *Little Jack Horner* all have good music; and with swing popularizing *A Tisket, a Tasket*, there is no telling how deeply the return to childhood may affect the American population as a whole.

With all this may be included such universal material as the French *Frère Jacques, Au clair de la lune*, and *Sur le pont d'Avignon;* the German *Lorelei* and *Du, du liegst mir im Herzen;* the Italian *O Sole Mio, Santa Lucia*, and *Spagnola;* and the Spanish *La Paloma*.

A rhythmically minded parent may even attempt Russia's *Volga Boat Song*, and every family repertoire should certainly include *Clementine, Love's Old Sweet Song, Annie Laurie, Ben Bolt, The Old Oaken Bucket*, most of the Foster songs, *Carry me back to Old Virginny, Auld Lang Syne, Comin' thro' the Rye, Loch Lomond* (in its pre-swing version), and *Believe me, if all those endearing young charms*.

Much of this music is available on phonograph records, but most of it can also be sung by anyone with a little confidence and the ability to carry a tune. Remember always that the baby is not likely to be critical.

ALL THE WORLD LOVES A LULLABY

Lullabies are important, for they will be remembered in later years. It has never been proved that children need the conventional type of lullaby to put them to sleep.

Probably *Frankie and Johnny* or the *Saint Louis Blues* would be just as effective (and they are not bad tunes either). Possibly even a piece of ultramodern noise would do the trick, for a baby goes to sleep not because of music but in spite of it.

However, there are lullabies that every young parent should know. My own favorite is the Brahms *Wiegenlied*, and lots of people seem to agree with me. But there is also a famous lullaby written by the French philosopher Jean Jacques Rousseau, with its melody largely made of three notes. There is *Emmet's Lullaby*, with its suggestion of a yodel, and there is the familiar *Rock-a-bye, Baby*. Mozart wrote a charming little song in which the baby is called a prince (*Schlafe, mein Prinzchen, schlaf ein*), and Max Reger created a similar effect in his *Mariae Wiegenlied*. The French *Dors, mon enfant* is another good lullaby, and Nevin's *Mighty lak' a Rose* should be put in the same class. Mothers of a past generation sang a pretty lullaby called *Baby's Boat;* and don't overlook Barnby's popular *Sweet and Low*, in which the whole family can eventually join, if they will learn the parts, for this harmony is not to be sung by ear.

There are still easier things, however, for the child or the musically limited adult—snatches like *The Farmer in the Dell, London Bridge is falling down, Goodnight, Ladies*, with its refrain of *Merrily we roll along*. Then there are the traditional rounds, also a foundation for future harmonizing. *Three Blind Mice* is one of the great compositions of all time, for it can be carried through by a voice commanding only three tones, and its full harmony has only two chords. It makes a perfectly good solo for any occasion in the first year or two of the average life. *Row, row, row your boat* is shorter and even easier, while *Scotland's burning* presents no insuperable difficulties. Several practical rounds are given on pages 98–100.

By the time a baby can understand something of the language it has been hearing and is presumably aware of rhythm and melody, its parents should command an impressive repertoire of songs, which their progeny will pick up in turn as rapidly as it is permitted. Children of three and four quickly develop the singing habit, with any encouragement at all, and their memories are far more retentive than those of adults.

THE INSTRUMENTAL ANGLE

If Papa or Mamma has made some use of these early years in personal music study, an instrumental repertoire is also a possibility, and even a slight knowledge of the piano or some other instrument can soon be shared with the child. Lacking such personal performance, the phonograph can still continue its work of creating listening habits and developing musical memory and the desire for imitation.

Children's pieces like Schumann's *Kinderszenen* and *Album for the Young*, or the *Children's Corner* of Debussy, even the simpler Bach *Inventions* (composed for his own children) sound well on records if no one in the family has mastered their interpretation. It would be a pity to

[23]

let a child reach the age of three without having heard *The Happy Farmer* or *Träumerei* or even the *Golliwogg's Cakewalk* of Debussy. Most of the music of Humperdinck's *Hänsel und Gretel* should be assimilated early in life, with particular emphasis on the beautiful evening prayer that occurs in the *Overture*.

Schubert's *Moment Musical* (the one that classic dancers used to do in cheesecloth with double flutes) and his *Rosamunde* ballet music may appeal to the very young. Tschaikowsky's *Nutcracker Suite* has the advantage of a good story, and even descriptive titles help to create interest, as in Bizet's *March of the Kings*, Gounod's *Funeral March of a Marionette*, and Rimsky-Korsakoff's *Flight of the Bumblebee*.

RHYTHM LIVES IN THE FEET

The primitive response to rhythm is characteristic of savages and children alike. It represents a physical reaction to music and its home is in the feet. Long before the human mind was aware of any distinctions of pitch, the regular tapping of a stick on a hollow log or some other form of drum had satisfied any basic desire for self-expression.

As soon as it was discovered that tighter drumheads produced a higher tone, and that shorter strings and pipes followed the same principle, melody entered into man's consciousness of music. The child runs parallel to the savage in this respect. He is only briefly satisfied with mere rhythmic noise. Several tones in a row, definitely related as to pitch, soon exert a fascination that is likely to be permanent.

MELODY AND MEMORY

Melody has an emotional quality which places it above the mere physical appeal of rhythm. Its devotees might be called heart-listeners, as compared with the foot-listeners, who demand nothing more than the insistent beat of time. But the chief significance of melody is as the memory element in music. It is by its melody that a piece is remembered, and popularity in music generally means little more than familiarity.

It is, therefore, advisable to interest children in tunes at an early age. They will make up their own tunes in time, but meanwhile they should hear as many as possible of the famous and permanently established melodies of the world.

Some of these have already been mentioned, and plenty of others will occur to anyone with open ears and an adequate memory. It is not necessary to descend to the current songs of Tin-Pan Alley, even though some of these have excellent tunes. Haydn, Mozart, Beethoven, Schubert, and Mendelssohn are all creators of simple but unforgettable melodies, and most of these can be had in recorded form.

Words are always a help to the musical memory, and if some of these tunes do not have words of their own, it is not hard to find some that will fit. For instance, the absurdly easy tune that Haydn wrote for the slow movement of his *Surprise Symphony*, with its interruption by a crashing chord, "to wake up the audience," can be sung to these words:

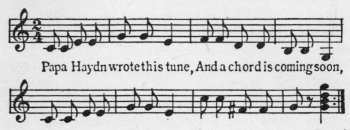

Papa Haydn wrote this tune, And a chord is coming soon,

It will be a big sur-prise, Op-en sleep-y eyes! Bang!

The familiar ABC tune, often sung to the words "One, two, three, four, five, six, seven, All good children go to Heaven," is generally ascribed to Mozart, and it is so similar to the Haydn tune that the words are really necessary, to keep them apart. Beethoven's best-known melody is probably the *Minuet in G*, which has also been fitted with words in various schoolbooks. Schubert's *Hark, Hark, the Lark* has a lilting appeal that will be obvious even to the youngest ears, and Mendelssohn's *On Wings of Song*, now familiar through the radio, has a similar charm.

GOOD TUNES CAN BE NATIONAL

The national anthems of the world are generally melodious and worth hearing, regardless of the sentiments expressed by their words. To the American patriotic songs already mentioned might be added

Columbia, the Gem of the Ocean, properly called *The Red, White, and Blue*. The piece originally known as the "President's March" (written for George Washington's inauguration) and later fitted with the words "Hail, Columbia, happy land," is a little too elaborate, but is interesting musically and historically.

The British Grenadiers and *Rule, Britannia* are both rousing tunes, and nobody worries about their words any more. The same is true of the French *Marseillaise* and the German *Wacht am Rhein* and *Deutschland über alles*. Russia's Czarist hymn, also known as *Hail, Pennsylvania*, and Italy's *Marcia Reale* and *Garibaldi Hymn* hold their own musically in spite of political changes. *O Canada* is a fine melody, and so is the Canadian march, *Soldiers of the King*.

Folk-songs are likely to be as strong melodically as rhythmically, and there are many fine tunes to be found in our own mountain and prairie music, mostly based on English, Scotch, and Irish originals. *Barbara Allen, Lord Rendall*, and other world-famous ballads exist in American as well as European versions, and of our less known folk-tunes *The Lonesome Road* and *Shenandoah* can be recommended. Even *Home on the Range* has its merits as an honest melody.

It is impossible to mention all the fine tunes that ought to be sung or played in every home, such as *Long, Long Ago, Afton Water*, the *Londonderry Air* and that other Irish melody, *Annie Lisle*, best known as Cornell's *Far above Cayuga's Waters* and sung by innumerable schools and

[27]

colleges. Old-timers like *Juanita, Upidee, Solomon Levi, The Spanish Cavalier, How Can I Leave Thee?* and the *Soldier's Farewell* have their place in every home repertoire and should never be forgotten.

THE PRIMROSE PATH TO PERFORMANCE

Most of this music is likely to be familiar to the average adult, even if it has not been learned in childhood. If you know even a fair percentage of it by ear, you can safely assume that it will not be hard to play some of it as well. Any grown person can pick up the rudiments of a musical instrument without difficulty, and there are also musical toys that appeal to adults as well as to children. Logically the toys should precede the real instruments, so why not devote a chapter to this important phase of music for fun?

BIBLIOGRAPHY AND NOTES

For stories concerning many musical compositions, see *Stories behind the World's Great Music*, by Sigmund Spaeth (Whittlesey House).

Hendrik Van Loon has published some of the best nursery tunes in his charming book, *The Songs We Sing* (Simon & Schuster), and there are various editions of *Mother Goose*, with and without music.

Many familiar songs are to be found in various collections, such as the song-books of Rotary, Kiwanis, and the Lions. Kenneth Clark's *Everybody Sing* (Paull-Pioneer Music Co.) is a handy and comprehensive paper-bound booklet, practical in every way. The Birchard books for community singing (*Twice Fifty-five Community Songs*) are excellent, and so are the variously colored pamphlets published by the Hall & McCreary Company of Chicago.

A valuable booklet, *Music and the Child*, is published by the Child Study Association of America, containing graded lists of pieces suitable for children of all ages and also indicating available phonograph records.

Jingles to fit symphonic music, and thus to aid in remembering the melodies, will be found in the author's *Great Symphonies: How to Recognize and Remember Them* (Garden City Publishing Co.). See also his new book for children, *Maxims to Music*, illustrated by Tony Sarg (Robert M. McBride & Co.).

FROM MUSICAL TOYS
TO INSTRUMENTS

SOME years ago that distinguished educator, Peter Dykema, head of the music department of Columbia University's Teachers College, appeared at a luncheon of the New York Kiwanis Club. He came armed with a great variety of musical toys—drums, rattles, horns, cuckoos, etc.—and he distributed them among the Kiwanians before beginning his talk. No sooner did these dignified business men have the toys in their hands than they one and all set up a terrific din of drumming, rattling, and blowing. Dr. Dykema watched them blandly as he let the noise go on for a few minutes. Then he raised his hand for silence.

"The next time your kids make a noise like that," he said quietly, "remember how you reacted to the same temptation."

In a short time he had organized the meeting into an excellent rhythm band, and with one good musician at the piano, they were able to play their new game as creditably as their own children might have done it.

I am strongly in favor of musical toys, particularly when they contain some of the fundamentals of actual instruments. A toy drum easily leads to a real one. A small xylophone or set of bells is the logical forerunner of a piano, and a toy trumpet, even when limited in range and a bit uncertain of pitch, can act as a stimulus to more significant wind exercises of the future.

THE PLAYTHINGS OF WAR

Is it a sign of the times that our toyshops are filled with imitations of the whole machinery of death by violence—rifles, machine guns, cannon, bombs, torpedoes, pistols, helmets, uniforms, and toy soldiers? The gangster and the murderer, legal or illegal, seem to be brought consistently to the attention of the younger generation through their playthings.

Outside the toy arsenal that forms so large a percentage of the current nursery equipment there is a Valhalla containing four deities—Charlie McCarthy, Mickey Mouse, Donald Duck, and Snow White— a wooden dummy and three series of drawings. Musical toys can be found if you look for them, but it is not easy to find them. There are two kinds—those that require no skill whatever, beyond perhaps the turning of a crank, and those that encourage whatever musical gift a child may have, and at least some slight initiative and control, for performance. The market is sadly lacking in toys that produce really musical effects, playing in tune and with a pleasing quality of tone, perhaps even with some degree of permanent stability. There should be miniature pianos, trumpets, saxophones, organs, and other instruments that would create enough interest and permit a good enough performance to lead directly to the real thing.

To a certain extent this is being accomplished by the manufacturers of musical instruments. There is a small reed organ of decidedly musical quality, already very popular with children. The tiny "butterfly" piano, with its double wings and short keyboard, goes far beyond the tinkling toy pianos of the past.

Adults and children alike should enjoy playing a "recorder," similar to the ancient instrument of the same name. It is made of wood, with holes pierced like those of a flute, but played from the end, and its tone is excellent, with an accurately pitched scale of two octaves.

PRIMITIVE WIND INSTRUMENTS

The ordinary tin flutes and pipes will always be popular, regardless of their musical effect, and a good deal can actually be accomplished even with these primitive instruments. There is much to be said also for the ocarina, or "sweet potato," which now comes in four sizes, making a complete quartet possible. (It was used in that way by four cowboys interpreting the song, *I'm bidin' my time*, in Gershwin's operetta, *Girl Crazy*.) The ocarina can be played quite musically, and is a popular member of the hillbilly orchestra, but it is primarily a most practical and nondisturbing toy.

Also heard in professional groups of the hillbilly type is the trombone flute, which consists of a double sliding tube and raises or lowers its pitch by simply extending or contracting the total length. Accuracy is difficult, and the quality is much the same as a rather hollow whistle, but it is lots of fun for young and old. The Hoosier Hot Shots, popular dispensers of rural music on programs of Uncle Ezra's National Barn Dance, make good use of the trombone flute, as well as of a washboard for rhythm (produced by thimbles on the fingers), a cowbell and several different auto horns.

The principle of guessing at pitch and sliding to and from a tone (employed by a number of singers, both amateur and professional) is illustrated by some percussion instruments, as well as such primitive pipes as the trombone flute. Chief among them is the Flexotone, a piece of flexible steel fastened to a handle and set in vibration by hammers attached to both sides. The player shakes the Flexotone to produce a musical sound, raising the pitch by pressing on the steel with his thumb and lowering it by relieving the pressure. Small Flexotones are used chiefly as rattles, but the larger ones produce a really lovely, ethereal tone, and used to be common in dance bands.

REVIVING OLD SAWS

Closely related to the Flexotone is the musical saw, which likewise has its pitch varied by the bending of the steel. It is usually held by crossing the knees over the handle, with one hand guiding the small end while the other starts the tone with a bow or a hammer. The beauty of the saw-music is in the changes of pitch after vibration has begun, giving the effect of pure air waves in musical motion. An ordinary crosscut saw can be used, although it is now possible to buy saws specially made for music. It takes a professional to perform on them really well, but the adult amateur can get plenty of fun in trying.

MUSIC IN THE AIR

A quality of tone somewhat similar to that of the musical saw and the Flexotone is produced by the Theremin, named for its inventor and still something of a mystery to the American public. Theremin, a Russian who came to this country some years ago, simply harnessed the squeal of radio and made it possible for people to draw tunes out of the air by shaking their hands close to an upright antenna. The closer the fingers, the higher was the resulting tone. Volume was controlled by passing the left hand over a coiled antenna below. It is, of course, impossible to play more than a single line of melody on the Theremin, and accuracy of pitch and rapidity of execution still present problems for all but the leading experts.

Mr. Theremin himself played the instrument only moderately well, but Clara Rockmore proved its possibilities in a recent New York recital, and Mrs. Walter Rosen has become a popular performer, combining charm and personality with solid musicianship. Mortimer Browning wrote a concerto for the Theremin, which Mrs. Rosen played at one of the concerts of the National Association for American Composers and Conductors. Carl Zeise, a cellist, used to play the instrument in the Philadelphia Orchestra, and it has figured in the dance bands of Vincent Lopez and others. The Theremin can be a musical toy for adults, but it has also proved its right to claim a place among legitimate modern instruments.

NO TALENT REQUIRED

The most encouraging thing about actual toys of a musical nature is that so many of them are made for children too young to do any real playing, but unquestionably sensitive to rhythm, melody, and harmony. There is a great variety of music boxes today, requiring nothing more than the turning of a handle or even rolling along the floor, but producing something that has a definite musical appeal. In most cases the response of the ear is encouraged by some colorful decoration, often enlisting the cooperation of the familiar characters of the nursery, right down to Mickey Mouse, Donald Duck, and Snow White.

Why should not musical instruments appeal to the eye as well as the ear? Part of the fascination of a trap drummer unquestionably lies in the variety and color of his gorgeous equipment, and bagpipers have a big advantage over ordinary piccolo-players. The instruments used by Shan-kar and other Oriental dancers always create a pictorial effect which the Occidental symphony orchestra completely lacks. Our toymakers are wise in their combinations of music and color and human interest.

Thus even the smallest toddler can pull or push a roller along the floor, listening to the musical pattern that emerges from it and at the same time watching a kaleidoscope of Disney characters or other colorful decorations. There are several varieties of musical tops, which hum a pleasing harmony as they spin. There is a splendid replica of a pipe organ, producing five different chords of fairly good quality at the mere turn of a handle.

A doll can be rocked in a cradle that plays *Rock-a-bye, Baby* automatically, and a rocking-chair produces similar music when either a child or a doll sits in it. Musical vehicles for pulling along the floor include a trailer that plays *Jack and Jill*, and a Donald Duck perched over a seven-keyed xylophone, which he plays mechanically from the ends to the middle and back again as he merrily rolls along.

MUSIC THROUGH PERFORATIONS

Perhaps the most elaborate of the music boxes is the Melody Player, whose crank handle causes perforated rolls to revolve, producing reedy but charming pieces, of considerable variety. A roll of *The Star-Spangled Banner* comes with each instrument, and extra rolls can be purchased at very reasonable prices, the repertoire including such favorites as *America*, *Dixie*, *Yankee Doodle*,

Home, Sweet Home, Auld Lang Syne, Silent Night, and *Carry me back to old Virginny*. Here, by the way, is the substitute for the phonograph or personal performance by parents in their children's earliest days, with twenty-four world-famous melodies quite adequately played with no effort at all, beyond the turning of a crank.

Music boxes and toys that wind up and go through motions, besides producing music, are also varied and practical. There is a mechanical drummer who should be an inspiration to any rhythm-minded child. There is an Aero Swing that plays the bugle notes, and a merry-go-round with a distinct pattern of primitive melody.

Christmas trees can be had that revolve and play *Silent Night* simultaneously. A musical lamp performs similarly to the tune of *Rock-a-bye, Baby*. Swiss music boxes are hidden in miniature pianos, which need only to be wound up. There is a gaily decorated hurdy-gurdy, topped by a dancing monkey; a village with moving windmill and animals, playing *Lightly Row;* and a "television set" which turns out to be a series of *Jack and Jill* pictures accompanied by their own traditional music.

One type of toy piano controls moving figures (Little Bo-peep and Mickey Mouse) above the keyboard, which covers an octave and is played by hand. A set of musical blocks produces a variety of tones when individually squeezed. But my own favorite remains a kazoo running into a board on which the loose-jointed figure of a tap dancer can be made to move rhythmically while one hums any good, lively tune.

[37]

When it comes to musical toys that can really be played, percussion leads the way and proves most satisfactory in the long run. Toy drums are almost as good as the real thing, and if they break more easily, that may turn out to be no great hardship. They have their pictorial side, too, which compensates for any possible lack of aesthetic tone quality. A drum or a rattle is the quickest and easiest reminder of our savage background, and the appeal of rhythmic noise is by no means limited to the very young. I have seen, at night clubs, otherwise dignified men whose greatest treat was to be allowed to play the drums with the orchestra. Incidentally, youthful drummers can develop their skill and a large repertoire by simply drumming with phonograph records or the radio. It is an absorbing game, though not exactly a quiet one.

BELLS, BELLS, BELLS

All the variations of bells and the xylophone appear in toyland, as well as in professional and amateur music. Generally they are dressed up to look impressive, sometimes with imitation amplifiers of the marimba and vibraphone type, but they generally play in tune and the quality of tone is not bad at all.

The Japanese manufacture a very cheap set of bells for children, but the American sets are worth the difference in price because they are supplied with little music books containing several tunes that can be played by the numbers corresponding to the bar bells.

[38]

These bells have a definite educational significance, in addition to their practical value as toys. Arthur S. Garbett, who directs and prepares the splendid Standard School Broadcasts in California, under sponsorship of the Rockefeller Foundation, has experimented successfully with simple sets of bells in the classroom and in the nursery, and believes they are the logical foundation of creative as well as interpretive work in music.

Toy pianos in general are not very satisfactory, and the various string and wind instruments have not as yet lent themselves to successful imitation. There are tin trumpets, saxophones, and trombones which look interesting and produce a number of tones with fair accuracy of pitch; but the quality of tone is not particularly musical and their life is likely to be limited, as the reeds give out and the tubes become bent.

HOME-MADE MUSICAL TOYS

If a household cannot afford the better type of musical toys, it is perhaps wiser to attempt home manufacture, and this in itself makes a wonderful game. In place of bells, one can always use glasses of water, partly filled, playing upon them with teaspoons, knives, or forks, or, perhaps more safely, with a lightly tapping pencil. The pitch of each glass varies even when it is empty, and the one with the lowest tone should be selected for the bottom of the scale. The higher notes are achieved by simply pouring in enough water for each desired pitch. This may be considerable trouble, but it is worth it.

With any luck, you should get at least an octave, perhaps with the half-tone steps of the chromatic scale, and this is about as much of a setup as can conveniently be handled by one person with two sticks.

Wine glasses generally give better tones than tumblers, but be careful not to hit them too hard. A thin glass will give out a lovely, light tone when the rim is rubbed with wet fingers. This was the principle of the old-fashioned "musical glasses" mentioned by Oliver Goldsmith, for which Handel once composed some special music. That loyal Princetonian, Paul Bedford, has a beautiful set in his home at Wilkes-Barre, Pennsylvania.

How many people know that the common or laundry pin is musical? If you hammer a row of pins into a board, with most of their length protruding, each one will give out a different musical tone when touched by the point of another pin. The shortest pins will sound the highest notes, and the longer ones will be lower in pitch. A complete scale can be worked out with a little patience and a good ear, or the series can be made to play a simple tune in the order of the pins, so that you merely run down the line without worrying about the order of the notes.

This, by the way, is the principle of many music boxes, with a central pin merely revolving and striking different metal pieces in turn. A pin-wheel organ can be made by setting pins in a circle on a board, tuned so that one round produces a complete melody. Then a revolving disk is set in the middle, with a pin protruding just far enough to strike each pin in the circle as the disk is whirled around. If you can make the disk revolve by means of a paper pin-wheel above, set in motion by blowing, you have a fine specimen of homemade, mechanical organ.

A drum, of course, can be made of any sort of tin can or wooden box. Down in Trinidad, where the natives make up songs about visitors on the spur of the moment, big oil cans are popular as the basis of the rumba rhythms. Gourds of all kinds make splendid percussion instruments, as is demonstrated in the typical Cuban, Mexican, and Hawaiian music.

BONES, WOOD, AND CANS

The clappers of minstrelsy's end men were originally actual bones, which explains why the interlocutor invariably called one of his wing comedians "Mr. Bones," while the other was "Mr. Tambo," obviously armed with a tambourine. Sticks of hard wood, rattled together make a good substitute for the Spanish castanets, and there are those who can get complicated rhythmic effects from a pair of tablespoons. Practical clappers, a variation of the Flexotone principle, can be bought cheap or can be made at home by attaching drops of lead to pieces of wood by flexible strips of metal, like the supports of an old-fashioned corset.

Boys of a past generation used to take the round top of a tin can, pierce two holes in it, and run a double string through them. After a good twisting, the tin disk could be made to revolve rapidly in two directions, by simply pulling on the strings with both hands and then relaxing them. A soft hum, like that of a musical top, was the result, kinder to adult ears than the insistent beating that any metal surface seems inevitably to invite.

Children can make their own xylophones out of wooden slabs knocked out of an ordinary soapbox. By whittling the pieces, they will arrive at definite pitch, the smaller and thinner pieces giving out the higher tones. Musical quality is naturally attained only with careful workmanship and specially selected wood, skillfully set over a frame permitting freedom of vibration. (A stock vaudeville trick is that of breaking up a box on the stage, immediately arranging the pieces in order, and playing a tune on them.)

MUSICAL BOTTLES AND BOXES

Another musical-comedy device seen in vaudeville and primitive shows is a "bottle organ," made of glass bottles of various sizes—hence, producing a variety of pitch—perhaps with a metal can or two for the lowest notes. They are strung on a frame, like the chimes of a symphony orchestra, and produce at least an amusing effect of limited melody. The bottle organ is obviously the poor relation or country cousin of the musical glasses.

Homemade banjos and other stringed instruments are good fun and sometimes not at all bad musically. A cigar box fitted with a neck of solid wood has been the traditional basis of such music. The strings can be of wire or gut, and even rubber bands have been known to serve in a modest way. The chief problem is to keep them in tune for an adequate length of time, and this can be accomplished by carefully whittled pegs. Bobby Edwards used to accompany his original songs in Greenwich Village with a homemade, cigar-box ukulele, and it sounded fine.

Wind instruments of a sort also can be made at home. Primitive musicians used conch shells and the horns of cattle for blowing signals, although they must have been of indefinite pitch. (Siegfried's horn, in the opera, would be rather helpless without the cooperation of the skilled horn player in the orchestra).

Youngsters living in the country generally know how to secure a piercing blast of sound from blades of grass held between the thumb muscles of the two hands. This trick contains the basic principle of single and double reeds, whose tone is due to the vibration of cane surfaces, either by direct contact with the breath, in a mouthpiece, or clashing together in pairs, as in the oboe.

A more musical tone can be secured by cutting a piece of cane or some other tubular wood, hollowing it out, piercing it with one or more holes, stopping one end, and perhaps inserting a cane mouthpiece at the other. The immediate result is a primitive whistle, but the whistle can be made into an actual flute or basic clarinet by careful workmanship in placing the holes and figuring out the best length of tube.

Many kindergartens, schools, and camps now make a feature of homemade musical instruments, arguing that children will be the more inclined to play upon the pipes, banjos, or percussion devices that they have made themselves.

Finally, there is the Pan-pipe of mythology, which can become a modern reality if one has the patience to cut a series of whistles of different lengths, building a scale from the longest to the shortest, and binding or gluing them together in the order of pitch. (It should be clear by this time that small surfaces and short tubes or strings produce higher tones than do large or long ones. There we have in a nutshell the principle of pitch. The interval of an octave above any given note represents a vibrating surface or column of air exactly half the size of that which produced the original note. Thus a piccolo plays an exact octave above the regular flute, and is exactly half its length. A violin string is stopped exactly halfway to produce the tone an octave above that of the open string.)

The boy who puts together several pipes, in the manner of the great god Pan, is on his way to the building of an actual pipe organ. In fact, he could easily make some actual organ pipes of wood, if he were a good carpenter and had some instruction from an expert. We used to buy at candy stores the graduated series of Pan-pipes, made out of licorice, and sometimes we could play on them before letting them melt in our mouths.

[44]

Aside from the fun of making your own musical toys, where the process is really more important than the result, there are only a few points worth considering in the choice of things that play and can be played with. Of all the category of music boxes and mechanical music producers it is necessary only to ask how early they can be introduced into the life of a child. As long as their music is not downright horrible, it will serve. Certainly, it is better at any time than idol worship or war propaganda. For children who have little talent and less power of application, the mechanical music-maker is a godsend and can be used right up to maturity, from a Mickey Mouse roller through all the music boxes that require no more than winding or cranking, to the final ideal of the radio, the phonograph, and the electric player piano, always with the assumption of a gradually developing taste that will eventually select by preference the records and the programs that represent music of a permanent value.

TOYS TEST MUSICAL TALENT

Musical ability and initiative can be discovered very early in the life of a child by exposing it to a few toys that permit a certain amount of personal performance and at least a choice between related notes and mere noise. If the child likes to pick out a tune or a harmony on bells or a primitive xylophone or piano, or if it begins to take an interest in the effects of closing certain holes in a pipe, there is immediate evidence of talent, and this can be encouraged and developed as far as the parents desire, long before a music teacher is even faintly considered and without any suggestion of turning a pleasant game into an exacting task.

Somewhere in the life of every child there is a danger point which must be successfully passed by tactful parents and teachers. Why do so many things that are the games of childhood become the drudgeries of adult life? Why does the little girl who loved to play at cooking and washing dishes and mending dresses so often grow into a woman who hates all those duties in her home? How can a boy who was once a good amateur carpenter resent the thought of doing the same sort of manual work for a living, or at least contributing such odd jobs to the upkeep of his own house? Why, above all else, do so many people who played with music in their childhood lose their zest amid the formulas of "practice" and "lessons" and "exercises," and end by being bored by all except the most brilliant performances, or possibly regretful that they themselves could not stand the drudgery that was demanded of them? Perhaps our adults, as well as our children, are badly in need of a trip to Musical Toyland.

BIBLIOGRAPHY AND NOTES

Some practical advice on the home manufacture of simple musical instruments is given in Mrs. Satis Coleman's book, *Creative Music for Children* (G. P. Putnam's Sons). The same author has a more recent book, *Creative Music in the Home*, and, for parents, *Your Child's Music* (both John Day Co.). Another of her valuable works is *First Steps in Playing and Composing* (Reynal & Hitchcock) and her *Psaltery Book* (Oscar Schmidt) treats a closely related subject. There are two books with the same title, *How to Teach Music to Children*, one by Elizabeth Newman (Carl Fischer) and the other by Clella Lester Perkins (Hall & McCreary). Also recommended are *Dulcimer Stories*, by Louie de Rusette (Sir Isaac Pitman & Sons, Ltd.) and the same author's *Music under Eight* and *Children's Percussion Bands* (E. P. Dutton & Co.). Two books on *Pre-School Music* have also been written, one by Floy A. Rossman (C. C. Birchard) and the other by Rose Ella Cunningham (Hadley Press, Inc.).

THE AMATEUR MUSIC MAKER

A GREAT pianist was quoted in the newspapers not long ago as announcing that those who could not play well should not play at all. A more snobbish, supercilious, reactionary, destructive sentiment was never uttered by any musician.

What this country needs, in addition to a good five-cent cigar, is a lot of bad piano players, accordion players, harmonica players, ukulele players, guitar players, and possibly saxophonists and trumpeters. I am not so sure about violinists and cellists, for their early efforts are bound to be pretty painful, even to themselves, and I admit that the oboe and the French and English horns should be left severely alone by all but outstanding musical talents. Drums and their percussive relatives, however, including the xylophone, can make their effects even in the hands of novices, and the technique of the bass fiddle has been whittled down to a series of rhythmic slaps.

Out of all this assortment of musical instruments, practically anyone can find something that is fun to play in a haphazard fashion. What would happen to the game of golf if it were played only by those who can consistently break a hundred? Would lawn tennis have survived if nobody ever stepped on a court without the assurance of being able to stroke the ball like a tournament expert?

Golf and tennis live on the vast army of dubs, not on the professionals or the top-notch amateurs. Baseball and football thrive because every normal boy at some time played one or both games on the sand-lots of his home town. The crowds at a World's Series or in the Rose Bowl have as their solid foundation those who have tried the games in their youth and therefore know what such supreme skill means.

The game of music seriously needs its sand-lot leagues, its dubs and rank amateurs. Standards of perfection are all right when applied to professionals, but they have no place in the average home.

Dragging in the ancient game of golf once more, it is hereby suggested that music teachers take a tip from the professionals attached to our various golf clubs. If a man wants to improve his game with a few lessons, what do they do? Would a golf teacher think of asking his pupil to stand on a mat in front of a mirror an hour a day for perhaps a month, swinging a club correctly but never actually hitting a ball? How long would he keep a novice interested with such a method?

The wise teacher of golf takes his charge out on the links immediately, tells him to try a few shots, and then corrects his most obvious faults as they reveal themselves. He may try to improve his form, but not by taking all the fun out of the game. The same thing is true of a good tennis professional.

Why did the old-fashioned music teachers insist on so many scales and exercises? Just what were they trying to accomplish? How many of their pupils ever came to play well enough to make a correct position and an impressive technique in the slightest degree significant?

LET'S BE HONEST ABOUT THIS

Is it rank heresy to suggest that nine-tenths of all the scales and exercises used in the study of the piano are a complete waste of time? They are worse than that, for they have definitely discouraged a multitude of pupils who might otherwise have enjoyed their music. The dreary formulas of "practicing" have actually put an early stop to the lessons of thousands who had the making of permanent music-lovers.

Technical exercises are absolutely necessary for those who intend to make a profession of music, as well as those who honestly wish to become outstanding performers in the amateur class and are willing to go through the drudgery entailed by their ambition. But they should be introduced only after it has become quite clear that a student has the talent, the industry, and the enthusiasm for music to stand such intensive training.

It is entirely possible to teach music without ever bringing in a scale or an exercise for its own sake. Problems of technique can be solved through the pieces in which they occur, and if a simple exercise helps in this solution, the wise teacher will find it easy to justify.

Playing a game of handball, squash, basketball, or volleyball is certainly more interesting than pulling on chest weights or exercising with dumb-bells, and the effect on one's health is likely to be quite as satisfactory. If music is treated as a game from the outset, equally satisfactory results can be obtained, at least from the pupil's standpoint; and the pupil, after all, is the one to be considered primarily.

There are several musical instruments which can be taught in such a way that the pupil is literally playing an actual piece of music immediately. This applies particularly to the piano and piano-accordion, where the tones are mechanically produced with little or no effort on the part of the player, and to the modest harmonica or mouth organ, which merely requires blowing, or at the most breathing in and out. The ukulele and guitar, if limited to chords alone, belong in the same class, except that someone must be around to see that they are tuned correctly. But the bowed instruments, like the violin or cello, and all real wind instruments—flute, clarinet, oboe, English horn, bassoon, French horn, alto, bugle, cornet, trumpet, trombone, saxophone, and tuba— present real difficulties in the mere production of a pleasing tone and are best attacked with the immediate aid of a good teacher.

[51]

The good old family piano is the instrument most likely to be found in a modern home, and is the most easily procured by anyone desiring a little self-expression through music. It is the most practical starting-point for musical performance of any kind and a solid basis for all written music.

So here is the way anyone can start right in to play the piano, with no lessons, at least to the extent of making something sound like a piece immediately. The first thing to do is to find one chord on the keyboard, and this can be used at once to accompany a complete melody. Of course you will have to sing or hum or whistle the tune, but the one chord will make it sound like real music. It is much better to start with chords than by picking out a tune with one finger.

HOW TO PLAY THE PIANO IN NO LESSONS

To find your first chord, look at the pattern of the keys. You will notice that the black keys run in groups of three and two, just like a full house. These five tones represent one of the oldest patterns in music, the pentatonic or five-tone scale. Play a group of these five black keys up and down, so that you will know how they sound. Each group shows the same relationship, no matter where you play it on the keyboard.

It is well to be familiar with this pattern of the black keys, for it occurs in most of the folk-music of the world. Perhaps that is why so many people think it is easier to play on the black keys than on the white. Irving Berlin is one of those people, and another was Charles K. Harris, who wrote that popular song of the nineties, *After the Ball*. (Berlin works out his tunes on a "transposing piano," which automatically shifts to any key desired, although the composer is always playing on the black keys.)

For the moment, the black keys are merely an aid in finding the tones of your first chord. Look at the pair of black keys nearest the middle of the keyboard. Put your right thumb on the white key just to the left of this pair of black keys. You are now on Middle C, which is as good a place to start as any. It lies just about under the left-hand end of the piano maker's name.

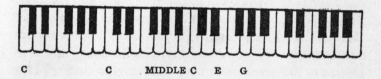

C   C   MIDDLE C   E   G

Now when your right thumb is playing Middle C, your other four fingers are necessarily over the next four white keys to the right. If you drop your middle finger, it plays E, and if you drop your little finger it plays G. Play these three keys one after the other, and then all

[53]

together. The result is a very nice harmony, which musicians call a triad (three tones in harmony).

When you play C, E, G, and then the three together, you get the opening of the famous *Blue Danube* waltz of Johann Strauss, which is built on this very simple pattern. But you cannot call this three-tone combination a chord until you have a bass note. So look down the keyboard to the left until you see another pair of black keys, and then put your left thumb on the white key just to their left, which is another C, an octave below Middle C. Perhaps you can stretch out the little finger of your left hand to still another C, an octave lower down— again the white key lying just to the left of a pair of black keys.

OH, YOU BEAUTIFUL CHORD

Now if you sound all these notes together, with both hands, you have a great big beautiful chord in C major; and the moment you have found this chord, you are ready to play a piece. It doesn't matter how often you play the chord. The chances are that you will keep time, for people do that by instinct. So play the chord as often as you like, as long as you keep time to the tune you are singing or humming or whistling. (Naturally the chord is only an accompaniment, but that is what gives it the effect of piano playing.)

An easy starter is *The Farmer in the Dell*, which everybody knows. The notes of the melody are given here, just as a reminder, and the chord is best played on every accented note. (The C's represent the chords.)

[54]

The farmer in the dell, The farmer in the dell,

Heigh ho, the mer-ri-o, The farmer in the dell.

Another tune that can be accompanied with one chord is the old round, *Row, row, row your boat*. This is one that can be harmonized by additional voices, if you wish, besides the piano accompaniment.

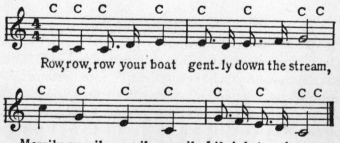

Row, row, row your boat gent-ly down the stream,

Merrily, merrily, merrily, merrily, Life is but a dream.

By this time you are all excited, because you are playing the piano, and you never thought you could. You can perform several more pieces with that one chord as the entire accompaniment. One of the best is the popular song, *Li'l Liza Jane*. If you do all the verses, you can vary the accompaniment by playing the chord twice as often

[55]

on some of them, and perhaps occasionally alternating the right and left hands.

Bugle calls and melodies can all be accompanied with this same chord, and there are plenty of them.

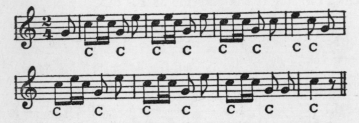

Now you can add a second chord and immediately double your repertoire. Keep the little finger of your right hand on G, where it was before, but move the middle finger and thumb down to the left, one white key apiece. Your middle finger is now on D, and your thumb on B. Change the bass from a C to a G (the white key that lies between the two lower black keys of the trio) and use the octave again if you wish.

Play the two chords alternately. You get the "sound of a great Amen." Forward or backward, the combination still spells "Amen." That in itself is something. But with these two chords you can accompany a lot of tunes, with the added excitement of changing from one chord to the other.

An easy one for a start is *London Bridge is falling down*. Notice where the change of harmony takes place. Any child can sing it and play the chords too.

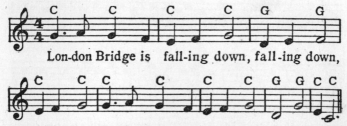

If you want to try a round with these two chords, take *Three Blind Mice*. It has three tones of melody running all the way through, resting on only two harmonies. Somebody may be able to play these three tones on the piano, above the chords, and any average musician can complete the round, instrumentally or vocally.

[57]

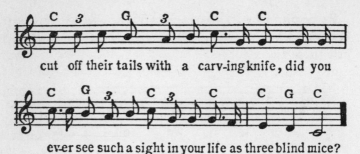

cut off their tails with a carv-ing knife, did you

ev-er see such a sight in your life as three blind mice?

There is a very important melody, by one of the great-est of all composers, that can be played or sung with only these two chords for accompaniment. It is the choral theme from the last movement of Beethoven's famous Ninth Symphony. You can even put words to it:

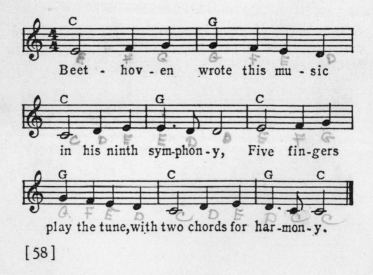

Beet - hov - en wrote this mu - sic

in his ninth sym-phon-y, Five fin-gers

play the tune, with two chords for har-mon-y.

[58]

Returning to a lighter type of music, here is the well-known refrain, *Merrily we roll along*, which goes well with just these two chords:

You can also play this in waltz time if you wish. Count one, two, three, in even time, and play the bass on the first beat and the right hand on the other two.

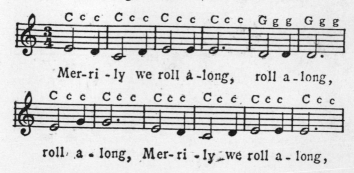

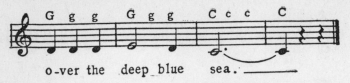

o-ver the deep blue sea.

(The capital letters obviously represent the bass notes, with small letters for the chords.)

This waltz accompaniment works also for a familiar folk-song, whose German original can be roughly translated somewhat as follows:

Lit-tle bird came a-fly-ing and a-sing-ing a song, So I kept right on try-ing till I played it a-long.

If you want to play the accompaniment of *Chopsticks*, just use these same two chords in waltz time, but be sure to start with the second chord (G), playing it for six beats (or two measures) before changing to the first (C). The simple, basic two-finger melody is given:

Finally, there is the gang song that almost everybody uses at some time for a public gathering, particularly popular with service clubs and conventions, *The more we get together*, another famous folk-tune, again with only two chords in waltz time:

[61]

By this time you ought to be ready for a third chord, and it is very easy to find. Simply move all your fingers and thumbs down one white key (to the left) from the second chord. Your right hand is now playing F for a top note, C with the middle finger, and A with the thumb. The left hand plays F for a bass, with or without the octave. You can call this the F-chord, using G for the second and C for the first. (The bass note gives each chord its name). Musicians would call the first the tonic, the second the dominant, and the third the subdominant; but you don't have to bother with such technical terms.

F   F   A   C   F

Try playing all three chords in a row, changing from one to the other until you are quite familiar with them. Then play the accompaniment to Foster's *Old Folks at Home*, like this:

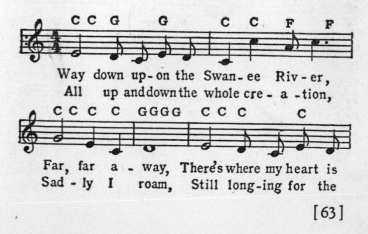

Way down up-on the Swan-ee Riv-er,
All   up and down the whole cre-a-tion,

Far, far   a - way, There's where my heart is
Sad - ly   I   roam, Still long-ing for the

turn-ing ev - er, There's where the old folks stay.
old plan-ta-tion, And for the old folks at home.

All the world is sad and drear - y

Ev - 'ry - where I roam. Oh, dark - ies, how my

heart grows wea-ry, Far from the old folks at home.

You can do *Old Black Joe*, *My Old Kentucky Home*, *O Susanna*, and *Massa's in de Cold, Cold Ground* with the same three chords, and in the same key. Other possibilities are *Dixie*, *America*, *Believe me if all those endearing young charms*, *Silent Night*, the Brahms *Lullaby*, etc. There is really no limit to what you can do with three chords, particularly after you discover that the same relationship exists in all the keys, and that you can play similar harmonies with A, B, D, or E as basses, or on the black keys, which represent the sharps and flats of the musical alphabet.

You will also discover that each chord can have the three notes of the right hand arranged in three different ways. Reading from the bottom up, the C-chord, for instance, could be played by the right hand as CEG or EGC or GCE, always with C for a bass. The G-chord can be played by the right hand as GBD or BDG or DGB, with G as a bass. The F-chord has as its possible right-hand positions FAC, ACF, and CFA, with F as a bass.

But by the time you have discovered this much for yourself, you are probably ready to go ahead with a teacher, and see how much you can actually accomplish. Naturally you can't do it all alone.

Every home ought to have a piano of some sort. They can be had in all sizes nowadays, and at all prices, so it should not be hard to acquire one.

But if a piano is out of the question, an excellent substitute is the piano-accordion or "squeeze box." Here you have the most popular of modern instruments, with a keyboard for melody and a "switchboard" for accompaniment. The tones are produced by reeds and bellows, so the accordion is really a miniature reed organ. Its portability makes it a practical asset to parties and picnics.

THE ACCORDION IS EVEN EASIER

What makes the accordion far easier than the piano is the combination of a shorter keyboard and a simplified bass, represented by a set of buttons. The best type of instrument for a beginner is the "twelve-bass" accordion, which has twelve buttons for the left hand, six producing chords and six the corresponding bass-notes. The keyboard, on which the right hand plays the melody, has a range of two octaves, from Middle C to High C, on these small instruments.

Accordions can be had in even smaller sizes, but most children and all adults can easily handle a twelve-bass accordion immediately. After this is mastered, the player can graduate to a twenty-four-bass instrument, then a forty-eight-bass, and finally to the big de luxe model that has 120 buttons for chords and bass-notes, and a keyboard covering well over three octaves. The Wurlitzer School of Music offers a practical plan of instruction whereby the beginner borrows an instrument until some progress has been made and then works his way up gradually to the best that he can afford.

Anyone can become a creditable performer on a twelve-bass accordion far more quickly than on the piano, and perhaps with more generally satisfying results. The method of approach can be practically the same, and a few hints for the self-starter should be sufficient.

The three chords already described on the piano are very simply produced on the accordion. Each is represented by two buttons, one for the bass-note and one for the harmony. Hang the accordion across your chest, with the straps over your shoulders, the right hand resting over the keyboard, the left hand slipped under the broad strap and poised above the twelve buttons, with the fingers free for independent action.

TWELVE-BASS ACCORDION SWITCHBOARD

Basses: (B♭) (F) (C) (G) (D) (A)

Major Chords: (b♭) (f) (c) (g) (d) (a)

The white key already identified as Middle C represents the lowest note on the keyboard of the beginner's accordion, although its position is actually at the top when the instrument is in place for playing. With the right thumb holding down this key (C), the index and

[67]

middle fingers of the left hand can press down the buttons representing the C-chord and C-bass respectively. (The button playing the C-bass is generally made with a slight identation, to aid the sense of touch in finding it.)

You can play this complete chord immediately by simply pushing and pulling the bellows in and out. This is best done in fan style, keeping the lower ends of the accordion together and letting it spread at the top. The left hand does the pushing and pulling while holding down the buttons. The chord can be played once or several times on each "breathing" of the bellows and the bass-note can also alternate with the harmony.

As soon as you have command of this one chord, and can play it in time, it will serve as an accompaniment to *The Farmer in the Dell*, *Row, row, row your boat*, and *Li'l Liza Jane*, sung as before, or played on an additional instrument. The second chord, on G, is just as easily found on the "switchboard," (consult the chart above) and the "Amen" effect can be produced immediately with these two chords. The right hand can play the second white key from the top (D) with the index finger, harmonizing with the G-chord. (Actually D is the next to lowest note in pitch on the small keyboard).

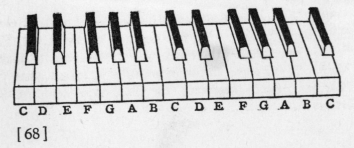

C D E F G A B C D E F G A B C

By adding a third white key, E, with the middle finger of the right hand, you already have the basis of *Three Blind Mice*. You can play the three melody notes, E, D, C, over and over, in that order, using the C-chord with E and C, and the G-chord with D. If you can sing the whole tune of *Three Blind Mice*, your three notes of melody and two chords will give you the effect of a complete round. Possibly you can get someone else to fill in the melody on another instrument, or use at least two voices in harmony.

MORE THREE-NOTE PIECES

For a second piece you can try the start of the old French folk-song, *Au clair de la lune*, perhaps using the following words:

Sailing in the moonlight with a pleasant breeze,
You can play this tune right, us-ing just three keys.

Three fingers of your right hand are enough for this little melody, with two chords played on the buttons by the left, as indicated.

Now it is not difficult to add two more fingers of the right hand, thus getting five notes in a row—C, D, E, F, G. Only four of these five notes are needed to play *Merrily we roll along*, either in waltz or in march time. (Capital letters represent the bass-notes and small letters the chords.)

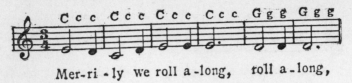

Mer-ri-ly we roll a-long, roll a-long,

roll a-long, Mer-ri-ly we roll a-long,

o-ver the deep blue sea. ———

You can then play the first part of Rousseau's *Lullaby*, using all five notes in the right hand (which means also all five fingers) and still with only two chords for accompaniment.

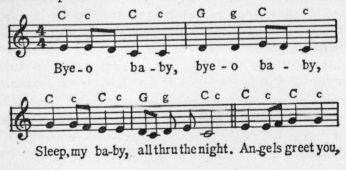

Bye-o ba-by, bye-o ba-by,

Sleep, my ba-by, all thru the night. An-gels greet you,

come to meet you, Guarding you till morning light.

Bye - o ba - by, bye-o ba - by,

Sleep, my ba - by, all thru the night.

The same equipment will serve for the start of Beethoven's great choral melody in the Ninth Symphony, already given for the piano (page 58).

This is enough for a beginning, and you can go on as far as you like, with or without a teacher, gradually including all the notes on the accordion keyboard and all the chords and basses represented by the buttons. The F-bass and F-chord logically follow the C and G, as on the piano. Then you can add B-flat on the one side and D and A on the other, and you have the possibility of playing in six different keys, with a melody range of two octaves, which is considerably more than that of the average human voice. The large instruments, of course, will take you far beyond this, including all the sharp and flat keys, minor chords, dominant and

[71]

diminished sevenths, and counterbasses. In fact, the switchboard of a full-sized accordion presents a complete and fascinating course in the elements of harmony.*

STRINGING ALONG ON CHORDS

The easiest stringed instruments to play are the ukulele, the banjo, the guitar, and the mandolin. The first three are useful chiefly for accompaniments, at least when in the hands of novices. The mandolin has gone somewhat out of fashion, but it still has its place as an instrument of both melody and harmony, the modern descendant of the ancient lute.

The four strings of the mandolin are tuned the same as those of the violin, and it provides an excellent preliminary to that far more difficult instrument, simplifying the fingering of the left hand by the use of frets, and substituting a plectrum or pick for the bow which draws the tone from a violin. The mandolin's tone is pleasing and not too loud, and combinations of mandolins and guitars are very effective. There is a famous plectrum orchestra in Cincinnati, conducted by "Hank" Karch, which has appreared on the Magic Key radio program and given many concerts.

Nobody should attempt to start playing the violin without a teacher, and only those with good ears should

* The experiments in melody suggested above can also be applied to the keyboard of the piano.

try it at all. At best, it is a painful process, going through those early stages when the tone sounds as if you were running a knife over a slate and every note is just a shade out of tune.

Viola players are generally violinists of an experimental nature, and many a cellist has also started on the violin. The four strings always have the same relative tuning, but at lower levels of pitch. (The top string of a viola sounds the same note, A, as the second highest string of the violin, and the cello is tuned a whole octave lower than this.) Double-bass playing is not particularly interesting, but exceedingly useful as the foundation of any instrumental group, with a modern jazz technique of slaps and jumps quite foreign to its classic traditions. It is a practical instrument for the amateur, if you are not worried about transportation problems.

TO YOU, MY UKULELE LADY

The ukulele is really a miniature guitar, with its four strings strummed by the fingers, or with a soft plectrum of felt or leather. The tuning makes it very simple to play two or three chords, and the key can be varied to suit the convenience of the performer. What seems to be the lowest string on a ukulele is really only a tone lower than the highest.

The four strings of the ukulele are regularly tuned A, D, F-sharp, B (with the A on the left or thumb side). It is quite easy to play a chord in D major, by simply stopping the top string (B) on the third fret, producing a top note D. The resulting chord is generally written as below, although the A actually sounds in the middle, with D's at the top and bottom.

Ukulele

A D F♯ D   A D F♯ C   B D G B

The change to the minor seventh or "blue" chord in the same key is made by merely stopping the first instead of the third fret of the top string, producing the note C, which is the minor seventh in the scale of D. A third chord can be played immediately by stopping the A string on the second fret, to produce B, and placing another finger on the first fret of the F-sharp string, producing G. The top and bottom strings now play the same note, B, but with the D and G between them, a perfectly good major triad is achieved. Several other chords can be worked out by the beginner for himself, and one short visit to Hawaii, or a few calls on a good teacher, will make him practically a master. These chords are generally indicated by diagrams on popular sheet music, showing where the fingers of the left hand are to be placed on the frets of the ukulele's fingerboard, and also giving letters and numbers to identify the chords for guitar as well as ukulele.

A number of modern instruments that look like banjos (with round, parchment-covered heads) are really mandolins in disguise, with their four strings tuned the same way—G, D, A, E. The true banjo, as developed among the Negroes of the South, has from five to seven strings, and is plucked by the fingers rather than a pick. Exponents of the real banjo are still fairly plentiful, and the instrument is worth learning for solo performance as well as in groups.

PLAY ON THE SPANISH GUITAR

The Spanish guitar has six strings, tuned from a low E upward through A, D, G, B to another E, two octaves higher than the bass-note. By simply plucking the lowest string with the right thumb, and the upper three with three fingers, you get an E minor chord. The index finger of the left hand placed on the top fret of the G string will turn this chord into E major (the G becoming G-sharp). A more practical chord, however, is that of C major, already familiar on the piano and the accordion. On the guitar, the bass-note (C) is found by placing the ring finger of the left hand on the third fret (from the top) of the A string. For the harmonizing triad above, the open G and E strings are used, with a C in the middle, produced by placing the left index finger on the top fret of the B string. The change to a G-chord, with the seventh, is easily made by shifting the fourth finger of the left hand to the corresponding fret on the lowest string (C to G), placing the left index finger on the first fret of the top string to produce F (again a parallel shift), and harmonizing with the open G and B strings. These chords can be played with a simultaneous plucking of the four strings concerned, or separating the bass-note from the upper three. This may sound a bit complicated to the novice, but it is really very easy after your ear has become accustomed to the sound of common chords.

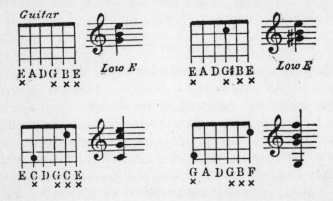

Good guitar playing, with both melody and accompaniment, is a real art, as has been proved by the great Segovia and a few others. While the instrument is a difficult one in its ideal performance, it serves quite adequately for a few chords of accompaniment in almost any hands. The Hawaiian steel guitar, which is primarily a melody instrument, offers entirely different problems and is best approached with the immediate aid of a good teacher.

Wind instruments, as a rule, also demand some personal instruction from the outset, as the production of the tones almost always presents some difficulties. This is particularly true of the flute, the trumpet, the trombone, the French horn, and the tuba, and such reed instruments as the clarinet, the oboe, the English horn, and the bassoon. The popular saxophone is a good introduction to the wood wind and there is now a simple instrument called the Saxette, which prepares the way for almost any blowing on brass or wood.

GONE WITH THE WIND INSTRUMENTS

Regular wind instruments are excellently taught in most of America's public schools, often in classes, from which the outstanding pupils soon graduate to the band or orchestra. Joseph Maddy has accomplished wonders in his radio programs teaching the playing of wind instruments, and the country is dotted with expert bandmasters who seem able to teach anyone to play some wind instrument in an astonishingly short time.

The lowly harmonica, or "mouth organ," is by no means a bad foundation for the future playing of more important wind instruments. It comes in all sizes and degrees of difficulty, from a simple octave of diatonic scale, requiring both blowing and drawing in the breath, to an elaborate chromatic instrument of considerable range and excellent reed-tone quality. Harmonica bands are now quite common, with Albert Hoxie of Philadelphia still the pioneer conductor and Borrah Min-evitch the outstanding virtuoso of the professional stage.

Instruments of percussion weave an eternal spell of fascination over human beings, particularly of the male sex. The savage made his first music on some sort of drum, and it is still the rhythmic foundation of every band and orchestra.

With practically no responsibility for creating a tone or playing in tune, drumming becomes largely a question of keeping time and exercising a certain dexterity with a pair of sticks. Anyone can drum in some fashion without any instruction whatever, but really good drumming requires teaching and plenty of practice. One has only to listen to some of the stars of swing and of the symphony orchestras to be aware of this.

Easiest of all is the pounding of the big bass drum, which demands little more than an accurate sense of time (unless you go in for juggling a pair of sticks with a lot of bagpipers). The side drum or snare drum has much more of a technique, and the various sets of drums and cymbals in a swing band, like the kettledrums in a symphony orchestra, demand both activity and accuracy to a high degree. Kettledrums (tympani) are definitely tuned, with their individual notes often changing in the course of a composition, which places them rather beyond the ordinary boundaries of percussion.

Playing the cymbals, triangle, tambourine, castanets, and other mere noise makers imposes no great strain on the musical intelligence. But an all-round percussion expert should be able to handle the xylophone, chimes, glockenspiel or bells, marimba, and vibraphone, all of which are closely related to the keyboard of the piano, and demand a similar knowledge of the scale, as well as the manipulation of various sticks and hammers. Percussion includes even the celesta, with its small piano keyboard and tinkling, ethereal tones. In fact, the piano itself is strictly a percussion instrument and really represents drumming of the highest type.

Children can easily get their first experience with instrumental and creative music through the simple sets of bar bells corresponding to five white keys of the piano, which are now approved and constantly used in public schools all over the country. The commonest model, played with one or two hammers, is constructed so that the five tones can be reduced to three for beginners, by simply covering the two at the top. The tones are numbered instead of lettered, and thus provide a permanent foundation for the command of the absolute scale, both by ear and by sight.

So it would seem that musical instruments and toys are not very far apart after all. They have in common the significance of a game, and they are intended primarily for the enjoyment of those who use them.

Select the instrument or instruments that you would like to play, and go ahead in the spirit of recreation.

One instrument may lead to another, or you can keep on experimenting until you find what you like most and can do best. There is no reason why adults should not pursue music in this simple fashion, and if they start early enough, there is no telling how far they may advance, for their own pleasure and perhaps that of others as well. The important thing is never to lose the feeling that you are doing it for fun.

BIBLIOGRAPHY AND NOTES

A charming and practical volume has recently appeared, the *Sing-a-Song Playerbook*, by Sam See (McLoughlin Bros.) with a set of bells, xylophone style, fitted into the pages. This permits a child to play immediately some of the traditional nursery tunes, for which numbers, words, and colored pictures are provided. It works.

There is now another device on the market, with a similar idea, called *Xylophone Playing and Singing* (Cole Corporation), which has the advantage of standing the instrument on a table in front of the player, with the notes held upright, as if on the desk of a piano.

Flutes, pipes, and recorders are developing quite a literature of their own, and there is an international association of pipers with their official publication, *The Pipers' Guild Handbook*, by Margaret James (Edward Schuberth & Co.). David Dushkin's *Fun with Flutes* is published by the Chicago University Press, and there is a practical booklet on *How to Play the Recorder*, by Wilhelm Twittenhoff (Associated Music Publishers, Inc.). The publication of similar material, in a practical form, is planned for the near future by Sprague-Coleman, sponsors of Alec Templeton's *Bach Goes to Town*, *Mozart Matriculates*, etc.

There are several good books for the quick study of the harmonica in its simple and more elaborate forms, including the Hohner Method, M. M. Cole's *Five Minute Harmonica Course*, *How to Play the Harmonica at Sight*, by Borrah Minevitch (Carl Fischer), and *How to Play the Chromatic Harmonica*, by Will van Allen (E. B. Marks Music Corporation).

HOW ABOUT MUSICAL VOICES?

There has been a lot of talk so far about musical instruments, real and imitation. But the universal instrument with which everyone is born, available almost without exception through a lifetime, is the human voice.

Vocal music may not be so important as instrumental in the long run, but it is certainly more practical. It is easy to argue that the most significant music is that which receives no help whatever from words, possibly none even from a title or an announced "program"— what the scholars call "absolute music." But words are tremendously important in catching the attention of those to whom pure music might remain a mystery. As far as young children are concerned, there can be no argument whatever. Vocal music should be introduced and encouraged as early as possible in their lives, and continued indefinitely through the years of maturity.

It has already been hinted that some children can carry a tune before they are able to talk. Certainly the gradual acquisition of a vocabulary can have a constant accompaniment of music. Singing is the one thing that even unmusical parents ought to be able to do to the complete satisfaction of their babies.

There is much to be said for the theory that everyone sings by nature. The best proof of this is in the fact that whenever inhibitions are temporarily repealed (perhaps by the use of artificial stimulants) the natural tendency of human beings is to break into song. When a cold-sober group of people are asked to sing, their self-consciousness usually has to be broken down by an insidiously beguiling leader, who encourages, cajoles, and occasionally even threatens them until they become natural and act like themselves.

THE PUBLIC UTILITY OF SONG

Song is an indispensable adjunct to church services, political rallies, football games, school assemblies, service clubs, smokers, reunions, boat rides, and wet parties. It is a physical help to boy scouts and soldiers when no instrumental music is available for easing the labor of marching. Sailors use it constantly to lessen the hard work of pulling on ropes. In fact, all folk-music may have originated in the simple necessity for a rhythmic accompaniment to lighten physical labor, and such primitive music must have been chiefly vocal.

Just because practically everybody can talk, and perhaps even sing in a fashion, there is a tendency to ignore the possibilities of the human voice in everyday life. We are willing to listen to a few highly trained singers, whose notes are often absurdly artificial, and we group untrained or amateur voices in community choruses or glee clubs, deciding that the whole is better than any of its parts. But we pay little or no attention to the obvious need of improving the average speaking voice, and we seldom encourage individuals to sing just for the fun of it.

There is much argument about "monotones"—those unfortunate people who seem unable to change pitch at all when attempting to sing—and it is a common boast, particularly among men, that they "can't even carry a tune." Yet it has been absolutely proved that monotones *can* be cured, by patiently developing their ears, and there is no such thing as a person who consistently and permanently sings out of tune. Miracles are being performed every day in our schools, largely by the association of the less musical youngsters with their more gifted fellows. I know of one man, with the added handicap of Quaker ancestry, who was considered a monotone and could not sing a note until he was in his forties. Then a good singing-teacher took him in hand, and in a surprisingly short time he was warbling a considerable repertoire and enjoying himself hugely. The inferiority complex may have had something to do with his earlier helplessness.

If you listen to any group harmonizing at a party, you will quickly realize that confidence is more than half the battle. One strong, accurate leading voice will hearten the others so that they actually outdo themselves and are astonished by their success. Generally they have already drowned all self-consciousness, and each new experiment increases their boldness. After a time the main problem is to soften the whole thing down and perhaps bring it to an end. This is most difficult if the host is one of the singers.

THE LAVATORY TEST

Another important psychological factor in singing is the bathroom. The lavatory test has proved again and again that man sings most confidently and successfully in the privacy of plumbing and tiling. There is a real physical help to volume and quality in such surroundings, an artificial resonance and amplification that persuades any normal male of his vocal impressiveness. But more significant than this is the psychology of privacy, which permits man to raise his voice without fear of interruption or criticism. The bathroom school of singing is universal, and it is a pity that its results cannot be made more public. There is an old story about a family whose members never learned to sing because there was no lock on the bathroom door. It is a vaguely discomforting thought.

Granting that everyone can sing, and should sing, a few suggestions are in order for the improvement of the speaking voice as well as the singing voice, and again the story goes back to childhood days. Even a definitely unmusical child will sing with little or no encouragement. By the time he is old enough to talk intelligibly, a number of the nursery jingles and simple folk-songs of the world should already have become familiar. Imitation of the parents would seem the most natural beginning of self-expression in song.

If a child shows no particular sense of pitch, there is no need to worry. He may actually sound like a monotone for a time, since his ear has not yet been developed, and he may even find difficulty in making the sounds that the sense of hearing would call correct.

The parents themselves may have the habit of singing slightly off key, in which case it is just as well to provide some instrumental accompaniment if possible. Good phonograph records always make acceptable models, and the tunes played by music boxes are usually in singable keys and sufficiently accurate in pitch. If the child has been hearing music from the very start of his life, it should not be difficult to arrive at fairly musical singing as soon as the articulate stage is reached.

VOCAL CRUELTY TO CHILDREN

Some of the songs written for children are pitched entirely too high, and there is a tendency in kindergartens and grade schools to demand a cruelly high range of the "piping voices." If a child's voice breaks, or falls into the tentative falsetto that always betrays lack of confidence, the chances are that it is being asked to sing too high for comfort.

A range of one octave is all that can be expected at the start, and this octave may lie most comfortably between Middle C and the C above. Experiment will soon show whether the child is willing and able to sing higher. Have you ever noticed how many people sing even the popular songs an octave lower than they are written? They are those whose confidence was shattered by the shrill straining of their childish voices.

Singing in the home does not require any carrying power, therefore a low range is entirely satisfactory for most occasions. It is only on the concert platform and operatic stage that high notes and trumpet volume are demanded.

The crooner at the microphone sings softly and at a rather low level of pitch, for radio always makes a voice sound higher than it really is. Perhaps the most significant art in broadcasting is this unique ability to transfer the intimate, confidential style of song and speech to unlimited audiences.

BING GOES ANOTHER ILLUSION

Mothers and fathers can and should be crooners in the best sense, for the word really has to do primarily with lullabies and home songs, not the distortions and artificialities that are so often associated with it. If children are encouraged to sing quietly and within a comfortable range, the effect on their speaking voices is bound to be noticeable in time.

Unpleasant voices, whether in speech or in song, are usually due to interference with the normal passage of the tone. Most people talk and sing "in the throat,"

[87]

and the first effort of almost any singing-teacher is to relieve this unnatural strain upon the vocal chords and "bring it forward." Hoarseness and "frogs" develop quickly if a person fails to make use of the natural aids to resonance and amplification of tone.

There are those who are fortunate enough to "place" their voices instinctively, and it is quite possible for untrained voices to sing naturally and easily, needing only to learn how to avoid fatigue. Too often a vocal teacher may spoil the natural quality of a voice in the effort to make it sing "correctly," and the artificiality of many "trained" voices is one of the major tragedies of music.

A great deal of bad singing, however, is due to nothing more than nervousness, which produces a "wobble" that is perhaps as annoying as anything ever inflicted upon a listener. Assuming that a singer has been well taught, or possesses a naturally well-placed voice, there is no reason for any lack of confidence, yet the vocal instrument continues to be the most difficult to control. A singer becomes short of breath through sheer fright, fails to reach a high note merely because of the fear of it, sags from the pitch on account of lack of concentration, and, in the wild terror that comes from facing an audience, generally forgets all the technique that has been carefully learned.

Real artists, of course, conquer these fears, although most of them admit that they are nervous before they begin. But if they know their abilities and have worked wisely and well to perfect their natural resources, they refuse to let themselves be psychologically handicapped. The best singing is that which allows its hearers to be consistently comfortable, under the impression that the singer is comfortable too. Any sign of strain or uncertainty or too obvious technique must be considered definitely a fault.

LET YOUR VOICE BE HEARD

There are a few simple rules that anyone can observe for improving the voice and keeping it from growing tired and hence unpleasant. These principles are followed in some form by practically all good singing-teachers, and they are unconsciously used by those people who instinctively talk and sing well.

The thing to remember is that the tone of the human voice merely starts with the vibration of the vocal chords and needs immediate amplification to become pleasing or even audible. This amplification is supplied by various chambers of resonance in the head, the chest, and the body in general.

If you fail to make use of these resonance chambers, it is as though a violinist tried to play on strings stretched over an empty frame, without a body to give his tones volume and quality. A pianist would be equally handicapped if there were no sounding-board under the wires on which the hammers fall.

Take a common tuning-fork and strike it so that it begins to vibrate. The tone will be almost inaudible, although you can hear it by holding the fork close to your ear. But place the handle of the tuning-fork on a board, right after vibration has begun, and you will hear a clear, mellow tone, often quite loud, for the board is supplying resonance and amplification.

The human throat itself has these qualities, but not enough for practical use. Above it lie the soft palate, the roof of the mouth, the tongue, the teeth, and the lips. There are also the nose, the frontal sinuses, and other cavities of the head. All these resonance chambers are supported by the chest cavity, the lungs, and the diaphragm, where the breath really starts with a muscular clutch. It is no exaggeration to say that the whole body enters into good singing, and when the singer stands on a wooden floor or in front of a shell, these artificial aids enhance still further the volume and perhaps the quality of the tones.

Probably the most important of all the resonance chambers is the nose, and it is certainly the most abused. When you hear a nasal tone and speak of someone's singing or talking "through his nose," you really mean that the nose has stopped the steady flow of the tone through its openings. Actually, nasal resonance is most necessary to good singing and speaking. The "nasal voice" is not making use of its amplification but letting the nose act as a barrier to the tone.

The best way to get the voice out of the throat and off the vocal chords is to put the tone deliberately into the nose. Take hold of it just below the bridge and sing the syllable "nee," making it sound as nasal as possible. Then try to produce the same sound without holding your nose. It is not at all difficult. The sound of ee is the farthest forward of the vowels, and therefore the best with which to bring the voice forward. That is why you hear professional singers constantly joking about "mi-mi-mi-mi-mi" (the natural vowel sound pronounced ee). They want to get the voice into what they call "the mask of the face." Keeping the tone well forward is their constant care.

Actually, the nose brings the tone forward if it is allowed free play without interference, and if you open your mouth and sing "nee" through the nose, you will soon get a mellow and well-balanced tone.

MUSSOLINI KNOWS ABOUT THIS

The final step in bringing the tone forward is contributed by the lips, which take on a funnel shape—sometimes called "fish mouth"—and thus add still more resonance to that which is already supplied by the nose and other chambers. Experienced singers always thrust their lips forward, but manage in most cases to look pleasant while they are doing it. Facial contortions are never popular with an audience, and again it should be emphasized that the best singing looks and seems natural, no matter how much technique may be hidden.

If you have succeeded in singing "nee" well forward, with plenty of nasal resonance, try the other vowels.

[91]

The nearest to the ee sound is ay, and after that comes ah, then oh, and finally oo, which is likely to be half-way down your throat by nature. If you are singing a comfortable ee, right on the lips, it should not be hard to switch to the ay sound, then ah, oh, and oo. (These are the natural, open vowels, and any other vowel sounds are merely modifications of them.) The shape of the lips in forming oh and oo will help to keep these vowels forward, and the sensation of singing all the vowels right up in the front of the face, without ever dropping back into the throat, is a delightful one, easily recognized and not really difficult to master.

MASSAGING THE VOCAL CHORDS

If your voice becomes tired or you have a slight cold, it is possible to massage the vocal chords lightly by softly singing koo-koo at a comfortable pitch. (You can always start your vocal exercises on a note that you find easy, and then work up and down the scale as you please.) The explosive consonant "k" is likely to give you a good breath attack. If you want to be sure that you are breathing from the diaphragm, just say the word "hook," hanging on to the final k for a moment and then suddenly expelling the breath. You will get the distinct sensation of a clutch at your diaphragm as you hold the k sound. If you practice this and get accustomed to the feeling of tightness between your stomach and chest, you will not have to worry much about breathing. The conscious control of the breath is often a handicap to singers, and too obvious breathing is always considered bad technique.

The consonant "n" is a good one for throwing vowels well forward, as it is made by the tip of the tongue just behind the front teeth. D is almost as good, originating in the roof of the mouth. M has the advantage of being formed by the lips themselves, and both m and n are "sonant" consonants, which can carry a tone and pitch of their own, leading right into the vowel tone.

THIS WILL SOUND MYSTERIOUS

After using the preliminary vocal exercise of "nee-ay-ah-oh-oo" on a single tone, perhaps at several levels of pitch, try singing "kaw-ay-ee-oh-oo" on the same tones. (All the vowels are always sung on the same note.) Then sing "nee-ay-ee-ay-ee," raising the voice one tone on the ay syllables. If you want to include your upper head cavities, sing the syllable "bue" as in "beautiful," very softly and as high as your range will permit, until you get a definite feeling of vibration in your forehead between the eyes.

These are all basic exercises that are distinctly helpful to the speaking as well as the singing voice. If you go through them just before you have to make a public speech, starting with plenty of nasal resonance, you are likely to find your voice clear and with a good carrying quality from the outset, with no danger of getting tired. Weariness of the vocal chords, with its attendant hoarseness, means that you have not sufficiently relieved them by using your resonance chambers. With a little practice, anyone can learn the trick.*

Children are now taught to sing correctly in most of our schools, and if they are fortunate enough to make the glee club or a mixed chorus, they are likely to get excellent individual training as well as group instruction. But parents can start their offspring in the right direction long before the days of school or even kindergarten, and adults in general can do much to improve their own voices for both speaking and singing.

OUR VOCAL SINS

Most American voices are pitched too high. In moments of excitement they become unpleasantly shrill. They also offend frequently by their loudness.

Usually it is not necessary to teach a child to make a noise, either vocally or in any other way. How to induce quiet is the real problem of most homes. The habit can best be created through the example of the parents. If their voices are harsh, loud, and shrill, their children will assume that this is normal and estimable. Soft, beautiful, refined voices are generally

* These simple exercises are part of the system first worked out by Dr. Frank Miller, who wrote an important book on *The Voice* (G. Schirmer), and applied in the most practical fashion by Miss Adelaide Gescheidt of New York, author of *Make Singing a Joy* (R. L. Huntzinger).

communicated from parents to their children, and this is commonly accepted as a mark of class distinction.

A mother will do well to moderate her own voice and bring out its best qualities when talking or singing to her child. She should adhere to a low pitch and encourage the child to do the same when he begins to talk and sing. Applying the principles recommended above, both the mother and the father of a family can develop their own voices and those of their children to a harmonious beauty. There is nothing more charming than to hear a whole family singing together, perhaps in three or four parts, and if the individual voices are of pleasing quality, such a performance may be artistically well worth while.

LOUD, BUT NOT VERY GOOD

Straining the voice should be discouraged at all times. There is no virtue in being able to sing loud or high, no matter what operatic audiences may indicate to the contrary. Certainly young children should not be permitted to sing or scream above their natural range, and the volume of their tones should be limited if possible.

Deanna Durbin is a splendid example of a naturally beautiful voice that has been well trained but never forced and that is today used in a simple and appealing fashion, without emphasis on exaggerated range or the tricks of vocal pyrotechnics. With radio and the screen ready at all times to amplify a small voice without loss

[95]

of quality, there is little reason for trying to develop the superhuman organs that were once necessary for opera and the concert hall. Wagnerian music-drama still requires them, but this is a very limited field, to which only a few are elected.

It is the perfect placement of Flagstad's voice, rather than its volume, that makes it pierce so easily through the big Wagnerian orchestra. Lawrence Tibbett has a strong, dramatic voice, but it is not "big" in the old-fashioned sense. John Charles Thomas also depends on quality rather than quantity, singing always with an impeccable technique. Richard Crooks has a luscious but by no means large voice, and Jessica Dragonette has won most of her popularity on the air, where quality and human appeal count far more than loudness.

VOICES CAN BE MADE

The careers of professional singers prove that good voices are definitely developed, regardless of their basic qualities. Natural freedom and beauty of quality must be taken into account, of course, but much depends on training and experience. Occasionally one even hears on the concert stage a completely "made" voice, used so artistically that it gives real pleasure. Such a voice was that of the late Paul Draper, father of the dancer.

It would be absurd to urge that all children be given singing-lessons. But it is entirely logical to suggest that parents and teachers alike should pay attention to the obvious faults and virtues of young voices, correcting, guiding, and encouraging their owners in every way possible. The pronunciation of the English language is also worth some attention, but that is too big a subject to be included in this book. Certainly we do not want to turn America into a nation of radio announcers, much as we might like to correct some of the slipshod—often positively ugly—English that is heard all over the country.

HARMONY IN THE FAMILY

Family or group singing is always more interesting if it is done in harmony rather than in unison. Two parts are enough to create an effect, and if three or four are possible, so much the better.

There may be one or two in the group who can harmonize "by ear"—by no means a rare gift. A female voice singing the alto part is an immediate asset, and the addition of a tenor or a bass, or both, will reveal new and unsuspected possibilities in the musical gatherings of the home.

Children can be given the feeling for harmony early in life by the singing or playing of rounds. There is no better way to become accustomed to carrying independent parts. The melody of a round should be learned first, by ear or note, after which it is a fairly simple matter to start each voice independently, the parts overlapping and making a correct though limited harmony. Here are some of the best-known rounds, all easy to sing.

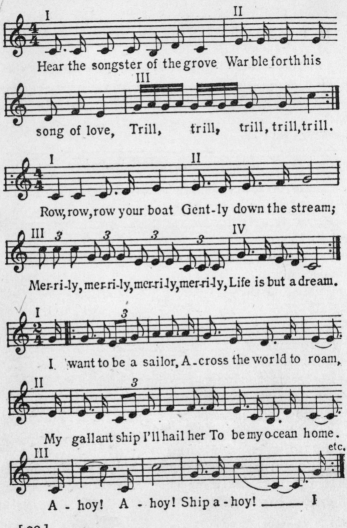

Hear the songster of the grove War ble forth his

song of love, Trill, trill, trill, trill, trill.

Row, row, row your boat Gent-ly down the stream;

Mer-ri-ly, mer-ri-ly, mer-ri-ly, mer-ri-ly, Life is but a dream.

I want to be a sailor, A-cross the world to roam,

My gallant ship I'll hail her To be my o-cean home.

A - hoy! A - hoy! Ship a-hoy! ——— I

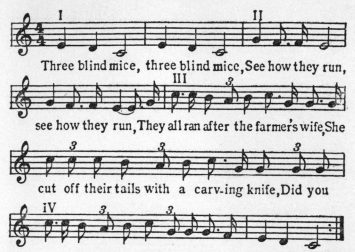

These last two are less familiar, but perhaps more musical than any of the others:

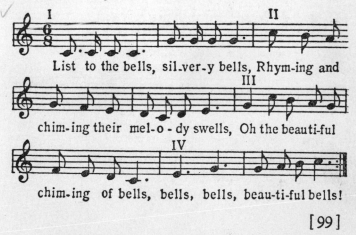

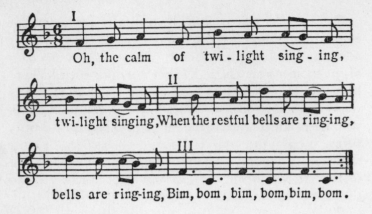

Oh, the calm of twi-light sing-ing, twi-light singing, When the restful bells are ring-ing, bells are ring-ing, Bim, bom, bim, bom, bim, bom.

HELPS TO FAMILY SINGING

By the time all members of the family are old enough to sing, some of them may have learned to read notes, perhaps in the process of playing a musical instrument, and these are the ones to be trusted with the harmonizing parts to be learned from a printed score. There is a vast satisfaction in being able to sing correctly all four parts of such a song as Barnby's *Sweet and Low*, one of the finest pieces of harmonizing in vocal literature. *Now the Day is Over* is an old family stand-by, and the trio, *Lift Thine Eyes*, from Mendelssohn's *Elijah*, offers most attractive but not too difficult harmony. With such a foundation, one may in time arrive at elaborate pieces like Pinsuti's *Good-night, Beloved*, with which the song-books are well stocked.

The term "close harmony" is generally applied to the efforts of a male quartet, and this type of group singing seems to be a law unto itself. The spontaneous, spur-of-the-moment masculine quartet does not even have to have the four voices implied by its title. It generally starts with a tenor, a "lead," and a baritone, with volunteers drifting in as the music gets better or worse. Before it ends, the "quartet" may have a dozen or more members, of whom only one or two are willing to stick to the melody while the rest disagree violently as to the proper harmonies.

THE BARBER SHOP STYLE

In such haphazard singing the tune is always carried by the second tenor, or "lead," with the first tenor moving along at least a third above. One such first tenor is enough to create the illusion of harmony. A low bass is usually harder to find, and he seldom stays down where he should, supplying the foundation for every chord. The most difficult part, requiring real musicianship, is that of the baritone, or first bass, who must always fill in the one note that the other voices may have overlooked. He has the most fun, however, for it is his part that completes the chord and gives it character and individuality.

Regular compositions or arrangements for male chorus generally give the melody to the first tenors, although it may wander from one voice to another. Glee clubs are now well trained in schools and colleges, and the

Associated Glee Clubs, representing industrial and business men's organizations, make it possible for any male to go on harmonizing with his fellows indefinitely.*

It is legitimate to take choral singing as the index to a nation's musical life, and in this respect the record of our own United States is not very good. Every town of any size at all should have its own male and mixed chorus, meeting regularly for the mere pleasure of singing in harmony. If an occasional concert can be given, there is cause for congratulation, but the rehearsals themselves should be sufficient stimulus. Unfortunately such choral organizations depend almost entirely on the inspiring personality of a leader, and there are not enough such leaders to go round.

I DON'T HEAR AMERICA SINGING

There was plenty of community singing during the World War, but after the excitement had died down people found too many other interests taking up their time. Bridge, automobiles, and the movies forced the choral society into the background. Today it has a hard struggle everywhere. You will hear some singing of current popular tunes in the movie theaters, to organ accompaniment, with the words thrown on the screen, and this is often quite successful, depending on the

* There is now also a Society for the Preservation and Encouragement of Barber Shop Quartet Singing in America, with O. C. Cash, of Tulsa, Oklahoma, as its guardian angel, and the author's *Barber Shop Ballads* (Prentice-Hall, Inc.) as its Bible.

personality of the organist. But general singing in groups seems to be regarded more and more as an old-fashioned amusement. It will have to be revived if we are to maintain our standing as a musical country, and the place to start the revival is the musical home.

BIBLIOGRAPHY AND NOTES

Dr. Frank E. Miller, author of the book on *The Voice* mentioned in a footnote above, also wrote a practical volume on *Vocal Art-Science* (G. Schirmer) containing more details of the system represented today by Adelaide Gescheidt. Pierre Key's book, *This Business of Singing* (Pierre Key Publications), is full of common sense. Lilli Lehmann's *How to Sing* (The Macmillan Co.) remains a classic of its kind, and there is much information in the late W. J. Henderson's *The Art of Singing* (Dial Press). Other good books on singing are *The Science of the Voice*, by Douglas Stanley (Carl Fischer); *Slogans for Singers*, by Florence Lamont Hinman (G. Schirmer); and *Plain Words on Singing*, by William Shakespeare (not the dramatist) (G. P. Putnam's Sons). They all disagree heartily with one another.

READING NOTES LIKE A BOOK

The notes of music are merely symbols representing tones, just as the printed letters in a book represent the sounds of words. Both notes and letters are intended entirely for the convenience of the reader, to let him know as easily as possible what the writer of music or words intends to convey.

Primitive music was not written down but passed on by memory, and there must have been language of a sort long before anyone thought of the possibility of using written symbols—even such pictures as the early hieroglyphics.

Notation, like language, has been a gradual growth, and it is just as silly to talk about substituting some new system for the old as it is to advocate an entirely new language when so many people already know an old one. In general the accepted musical notation is logical enough, and while it can be supplemented by the use of numbers and the sol-fa system of syllables, it is not likely to undergo any fundamental change in future. The only problem today is to find ways of writing down the noises that are definitely outside the accepted musical scale, and that problem can be left to the ultra-modernists to solve.

If one grasps the principles of note reading and writing, the mechanical details become very simple. A few facts have to be learned, and after that it is a mere question of practicing and using this knowledge until it becomes automatic.

HOW HIGH AND HOW LONG?

The two important things that the reader of music must know about every note are its pitch and its duration in time. The composer can easily indicate whether it is to be played loud, soft, or medium (using the Italian symbols—*f* for *forte*, or loud; *ff* for very loud; *p* for *piano*, or soft; *pp* for very soft; and possibly *mf* for moderately loud). He can write at the start of a composition what instrument is to play each part. But the individual notes must show by their size, shape, and position just what tones they represent and how long each of them is to be sustained.

Notation is best learned at the keyboard of a piano, where the scale is very clearly shown by the pattern of the black and white keys. If you strike any white key and play upwards (to the right), striking each white key in turn, you will discover that the eighth white key will duplicate the one on which you started, both in its relation to the black keys and in its tone, which is exactly an octave higher. Actually, you will thus be playing one of the ancient Greek modes or scales, which were later adapted to the Gregorian music of the church.

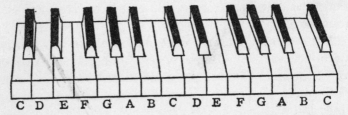

The diagram of the keyboard makes clear the progression of the letters representing the notes of the scale. There are only seven of them—A, B, C, D, E, F, and G. The eighth note above A will be A again, but an octave higher. The five black keys (which make up a grand total of only twelve half-tones within the limits of one octave) take their names from the adjoining white keys, each being known as the sharp of the white key below it and the flat of the white key above. Thus the black key between A and B is both A-sharp and B-flat, depending upon the convenience of the reader. Notice that B and C are only half a tone apart, and so are E and F, so there are no black keys between these white ones.

Notes are written on a staff of five lines and four spaces, representing different levels of pitch. Obviously, that allows for only nine different notes, and even if you perch another on top and hang an extra one under the bottom line, you have only eleven, which is less than an octave and a half. Of course all these notes can be sharped or flatted by the addition of a simple sign, and that brings up the total considerably. But the reader would still be handicapped if he had to read all the notes of music from a single staff of five lines and four spaces.

Theoretically, notes can be added above and below without limit, by simply writing short lines (known as "leger lines") through or above or below the notes that sound higher or lower than the extremes of the staff. But even this has its drawbacks, as it soon becomes impossible to keep track of the extra lines. (Remember that all notation is merely for the convenience of the reader.)

So music uses regularly at least two "clefs," to indicate a higher or lower level of pitch represented by an entire staff. Roughly speaking, most of the notes above Middle C are written in the "treble clef," and most of those below Middle C in the "bass clef." (There are several intermediate clefs, used chiefly in orchestral music, but they are of no significance to the novice in note reading. Treble and bass are sufficient for all ordinary purposes.)

NOTATION IN THE TREBLE CLEF

NOTATION IN THE BASS CLEF

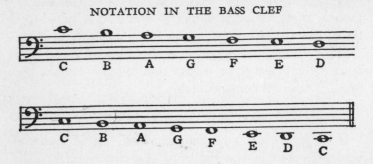

Thus Middle C again becomes a most important starting-point, and may really be considered the connecting link between the two common clefs. Written in the treble clef, it appears as the note crossed by the first leger line below the staff.

In the bass clef, Middle C is the first note crossed by a leger line above the staff, so it may be said to lie directly between the two. Nothing could better illustrate the convenience of using two clefs. The moment either one shows any danger of becoming cluttered up with extra leger lines, it runs logically and easily into the other.

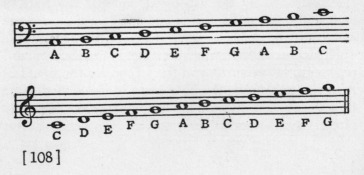

[108]

Of course the highest notes in the treble clef and the lowest in the bass are bound to run into a lot of leger lines. But if there is a passage of any length in a very high or a very low range, it is always possible to write it an octave lower or higher and simply use the sign 8*va*⌒⌒⌒for its continuation.

TWO CLEFS ARE ENOUGH

It is surprising how much printed music lies conveniently within the limits of the two familiar clefs. Even a professional soprano cannot sing far above the top of the treble staff, and the average bass voice is content to reach the F at the bottom of the bass. Music for the violin and most other solo instruments, as well as for soprano, alto, and tenor voices, is regularly written in the treble clef. Piano music uses both clefs— the treble for the right hand and the bass for the left— and again it is surprising how seldom it is necessary to go far beyond the lines and spaces of the staff.

These lines and spaces should, therefore, be thoroughly learned, first in the treble and then in the bass clef (indicated by the decorative signs at the start of each staff). The notes within and upon them are definite and constant in their pitch, representing always the same number of vibrations per note. ("Standard pitch" represents 440 vibrations to the second for the sound of A in the treble clef, the note lying in the second space from the bottom. There are people who possess "absolute pitch," which enables them to call off a note without seeing it struck on the keyboard. "Comparative pitch" is far easier, and can be developed by practice, since the ear should be able to figure out the letter of any succeeding note after hearing one identified.)

The sign of a sharp (#) always raises the pitch of a note by half a tone, and the sign of a flat (♭) lowers it by the same amount. If one or more notes are to be played sharp or flat all the way through a piece, or a section of a piece, this is indicated by a "signature" at the start, which saves writing out the "accidentals" each time. A sharp or a flat can be canceled by writing a "natural" sign (♮) if the note is in the same measure. If it occurs in a later measure, the cancellation is automatic. It will be found that every major key except that of C requires at least one note to be sharped or flatted throughout.

TONES IN TIME

Once you are thoroughly familiar with the relative pitches of the notes in the treble and bass clefs, you merely have to learn to recognize their duration in time. Music in general is metrical, just like poetry. There are definite accents, and where poetry speaks of "feet," music refers to "measures."

A measure of music (often called a "bar," because it is marked off by vertical bars crossing the staff) is nothing more than a convenient unit for the grouping of notes in time. The first note of every measure has the strongest accent within that measure, generally known as the "down-beat." In waltz time, for instance, there are three beats to a measure, with the first always getting the accent. March time may have two or four beats, but the first is always the most important, with the third perhaps getting a secondary accent in a group of four.

COMMON TIME MARCHES ON

This grouping of time beats in fours is so general that it is often called "common time," and because of it the quarter-note has become the accepted unit of notation, as far as time is concerned. The "time signature" at the start of a piece indicates how many quarter-notes there are to a measure by simply putting a numeral—2, 3, or 4—above the number 4 which represents the quarter-note as the basic unit. It looks like a fraction, and it is. Some fast music is written with the eighth-note as its unit of time, and some very slow music still uses half-notes as units; but the vast majority of compositions show their time in terms of quarter-notes.

By simple arithmetic it takes four quarter-notes to make a whole note, and two quarters to make a half-note. A whole note is, therefore, four times as long as a quarter-note and twice as long as a half-note, which in turn is twice as long as a quarter-note. You don't need anything longer than a whole note in music, for if you want a tone to last more than four beats, you simply write an additional note and tie it on with a curved line, to show that the sound is continuous.

But there are often shorter notes than quarters, chiefly eighths and sixteenths. An eighth-note is half the length of a quarter, and a sixteenth is half as long as an eighth. So a measure of common time (four-four) could contain one whole note or two halves or four quarters or eight eighths or sixteen sixteenths, or any combination of these time values that totaled four beats or quarters.

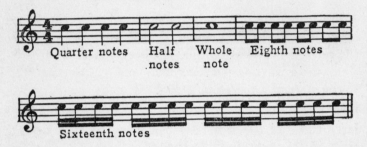

Quarter notes   Half .notes   Whole note   Eighth notes

Sixteenth notes

A dot placed after a note increases its length by one-half its original value. A half-note, for instance, is lengthened to three beats instead of two when a dot is placed after it; and this is quite common, particularly in waltz time, where there are three beats to a measure, amounting to a time value of three quarter-notes. (A note could also be lengthened by simply tying on an extra note of the same pitch, and this is often done).

THE REST IS HELPFUL

If a composer wishes to indicate a pause between notes or to fill out a measure of time without sustaining a note, he uses "rests." There is a rest corresponding in time value to each of the notes, from the whole note to the sixteenth, or even the smaller units that are possible. You can even add a dot to a rest and thus increase its length by half its original value.

In learning to read notes, it is advisable to count out loud at first, and even experienced musicians—particularly those in dance bands—can often be seen beating time with their feet. Eventually, however, keeping time should become entirely mental. It is not really difficult, particularly if one remembers that the downbeat always comes at the start of a measure.

ALL MARCH OR WALTZ TIME

If you are familiar with waltz time (three-four) and march time (two-four and four-four), you will find yourself able to read most of the music of the world. But it is quite easy to add the eighth-note as a unit of measurement, particularly for six-eight time, which is often used for marches. This means merely that each measure contains six beats, each representing an eighth-note. Actually they divide into two sets of three each, and such time can easily be beaten as two-four, using the first set of three eighths for the down-beat and the second for the up-beat.

To simplify an accompaniment or perhaps a melody which groups notes in threes, it is possible to write not only in six-eight but also in nine-eight and twelve-eight time. These are all known as "compound time,"

as compared with the simple two, three, and four beats to a measure. Nine eighths are really three groups of three each, amounting to a slow waltz time, and twelve eighths similarly represent four groups of three each, or a slow four-four beat. A time signature of three eighths is frequently used (especially in mazurkas) to indicate a triple beat somewhat faster than waltz time. Modern music also shows an occasional irregular beat, such as five-four or seven-eight, but it is not necessary to worry about those. Actually, they represent merely an alternation of the multiples of two and three that are traditional in music.

When you can tell the pitch and the duration of any note at sight, you are potentially a reader of music, and the rest is just a matter of practice, like any reading. There are certain signs and directions in music which can be gradually picked up. Unfortunately we have inherited the general directions for speed, etc., from the Italian language, and few composers have the courage to write down what they mean in plain English. (Percy Grainger is a notable exception).

The following terms are the ones most likely to be encountered in an ordinary piece of music: *Presto*—very fast; *Allergo*—fast; *Allegretto*—fairly fast; *Moderato*—moderately fast or slow; *Andante*—rather slow; *Adagio*—quite slow; *Largo*—very slow; *Accelerando*—increasing in speed; *Ritardando*—growing slower; *Crescendo*—growing louder; *Diminuendo*—growing softer; *Sforzando*—with a sudden accent; *Da capo*—going back to the beginning; *Fine*—the end; *Tutti*— all the instruments; *Tacet*—be silent; *A tempo*—in the same time as before.

If a note is to be held beyond its regular time value, it may be indicated by a *Fermata* or "bird's-eye" placed above it. A dot over a note shows that it is to be played "staccato," very short, in a brittle fashion. "Legato," or the smooth, sustained style of playing, is indicated by curved lines running above the notes to be played thus. Fox-trot time is frequently written "alla breve," meaning that the beats are counted two instead of four to a measure, and indicated by a vertical line through the C that shows the Common Time. There are various ways of showing trills, turns, and other ornaments of music. An increase or diminishing of loudness can also be shown by a simple wedge, which opens toward the louder sound and closes at the soft end. A special accent may be indicated by a small wedge placed directly over the note affected.

USE THE NOTES IN THIS BOOK

Check the information above with some of the illustrations in other parts of this book. You will find that reading music is not at all hard. Start by reading things that you already know fairly well by ear, so that the sounds will not be completely strange to you. After a while you will find that any notes at all form themselves into logical combinations of pitch and time. You do not even have to play them on an instrument or sing them, any more than you have to read out loud in order to grasp what is on a printed page. You will get the habit of hearing mentally a whole measure or phrase at a time, just as you read not individual words but sentences or at least phrases and clauses. Then you will wonder why you deliberately shut yourself off from the literature of music for so long. The person who boasts of not being able to read notes is like one who considers it a virtue not to be able to read a newspaper, a magazine, or a book. Such a person can hear plenty of interesting things, but it would be fun to be able to read them too, besides saving a lot of time.

GAMES AND TRICKS WITH MUSIC

I<small>F A</small> family includes even one fairly able musician, particularly a pianist, there are endless opportunities for musical games and diversions in which all can take part. Some of these tricks are possible even without talented leadership, and they may serve to stimulate the interest of those who are not likely to make music for its own sake but can be caught by some novelty of approach or an appeal to their general mentality.

For those who have heard considerable music, but do not necessarily play, a simple but amusing game is possible with patterns of rhythm. The one who is "it" taps out a tune on the table or by clapping the hands, and the others try to guess what piece he has in mind. Only a few measures are necessary, the taps representing the notes of the melody, but only in their rhythmic significance, without any change of pitch.

Thus the start of Beethoven's *Fifth Symphony* (which actually represents "Fate knocking at the door") would be given as three short taps and a long one, twice in succession. That would be a fairly easy one to guess for anybody who had heard the symphony.

What makes such a game exciting is that so many tunes begin with the same pattern of rhythm, and identification may thus be quite difficult, even though the pieces are familiar. For instance *Yankee Doodle*, the old ABC tune, and the slow movement of Haydn's *Surprise Symphony* all begin with exactly the same rhythmic pattern—six short tones followed by a long one—and in two of them it is immediately repeated without change. *Long, Long Ago*, some hymn tunes, and the Schubert *Military March* all start with a long tone followed by two short ones, and this pattern is repeated at least three times. The identity of rhythmic pattern at the opening of the Chopin *Funeral March* and the Lohengrin *Wedding March* of Wagner has often been pointed out.

HAVING WONDERFUL TIME

Another way to capitalize the universal sense of time is to get up an impromptu rhythm band. When actual instruments or musical toys of the type of drums, rattles, bells, xylophones, etc., are available, you can obtain some fine effects by giving each person a definite pattern to play, with no other responsibility than to keep time. Haydn carried out the principle in his *Toy Symphony* on a fairly high musical plane, writing out definite parts for a number of absurd instruments, including the cuckoo-call, a tin trumpet, and the imitation of a German quail, using a pianist and a violinist to provide the real musical basis.

People at a party can have just as much fun by using household utensils as the foundation of a rhythm band. After refreshments have been served, it is not hard to adapt the combinations of spoons, knives, forks, plates, and glasses to various patterns of rhythm, as long as a strongly defined beat is maintained by one or more adequate musicians or by a phonograph record or the radio. A pencil tapping on a parchment lamp-shade makes a pleasing drum-beat, not too loud. Even a cocktail shaker, with its remaining ice, can be turned into a practical rattle. Sandpaper or its equivalent is not hard to procure, and a fly swatter or a whisk broom playing on a suitcase has proved its rhythmic value even in professional bands.

YOU SING INTO IT

Melody can always be supplied by the faithful kazoo, which comes in many convincing shapes, and the stationery stores and novelty shops sell a wide variety of horns, rattles, and noise-makers of all kinds. Tissue paper on a comb is still an excellent substitute for the kazoo, and the great Franz Schubert himself did not disdain to use such a makeshift in his lighter moments, burlesquing his own *Erlking* music.

In a pinch, it is the invaluable phonograph record that makes such impromptu music possible to-day. Any lively tune with a definite beat will do, such as *Dixie*,

[119]

Turkey in the Straw, or a Strauss waltz. Up-to-date popular tunes are sure to provide a good rhythmic basis, and ambitious players can even aim at some of the effects of swing. Amateur trap drummers have already been urged to experiment with a rhythmic accompaniment to records, and anyone can also have a wonderful time playing orchestral conductor to a record, going through all the motions, with the assurance that no player will miss his beat. A good leader is always a help to the home rhythm band; and if he is familiar with a record in advance and knows the possibilities of its rhythmic patterns, he will have no difficulty in whipping his extemporaneous musicians into shape. With someone at the piano who really knows his business, the whole thing becomes still easier, and very little rehearsing should be needed for a performance that will at least prove amusing.

AND THE ANGELS SING

If a party is more inclined toward song than instrumental music, there are plenty of stunts and experiments from which to choose. Actual "close harmony" is perhaps most satisfying, but if the crowd contains no natural harmonizers, there are other ways of securing similar effects. The singing of rounds has already been recommended, and this is comparatively easy for any group of individuals able to carry a tune and keep time. A battle of melodies is another way of securing rather crude harmony quite in the tradition of the ancient polyphonic music, which merely made one melody harmonize with others. *The Long, Long Trail* goes quite well with *Keep the Home Fires Burning*, if you start the second song after two words of the first have been sung, representing an up-beat.

The old combination of *The Spanish Cavalier* and *Solomon Levi* is still a possibility (there are plenty of people alive who know the tunes) and it is fairly well known that *Old Folks at Home* can be sung as a counter-melody to the first part of Dvorak's *Humoresque*, which may be hummed or whistled if nobody can play it on an instrument. It may be a surprise to find that *Yankee Doodle* and *Dixie* work together splendidly, at least for the first section, and an ambitious countersinger can even add *Home Sweet Home* and still keep up some sort of harmony.

THIS ONE IS EASY

An amusing imitation of folk-music in three different languages can be given by any group of at least four voices, three parts acting as a chorus (carrying the "burden") and the fourth as a soloist. The top voices sing "litum," which might be Scandinavian for "When good fellows get together." The second part is sung to the words "illi buscum," meaning perhaps "Shall we join the ladies?" (The answer is "No.") The lowest part sings "boolah," which is College for "Yale will win."

These three parts harmonize on the notes indicated below. Rehearse each part separately, in a steady time. Then bring them in one after the other until they are singing a nice chord, not too loud, repeating their nonsensical words over and over. Then the solo voice comes in, with even more nonsensical effect. At the end the leader spreads his arms and everybody holds on to a final "Ah!" with one or more top voices going up to the octave to complete the chord. Here is the way it works out in notation:

Li-tum li-tum   Il-li bus-cum   Boo-lah, boo-lah

Ah li   ah li ___ ah li   ah li ah ___ ah li   ah li ah li,

ah li ah li_   ah li ah li   ah li ah li   ah! ___

The music books are full of "stunt songs" that anybody can pick up very quickly. Outstanding are the French Canadian *Alouette*, which depends mostly on a good leader; *Macdonald's Farm*, with its killingly funny imitations of barn-yard animals; the fabulous *Schnitzelbank*, which really needs a chart with words or pictures; *Johnny Schmoker*, which goes in for instrumental imitations, very popular with glee clubs; and such innocent absurdities as the *Prairie Flower* and *Gymnastic Relief* (to the tune of *Till we meet again*), found in the song-books of Rotary, Kiwanis, and the Lions, and used at many a club luncheon to offset the possible dullness of a speaker.

A good way to learn the notes of music and the relationships of the absolute scale is by playing games that turn letters and numbers into melodies and vice versa. As already indicated, the musical alphabet has only seven letters, from A to G inclusive, as against twenty-six in the regular English alphabet. It is really quite easy to learn.

"Musical Alphabet" can be played in two ways. One is to have someone at the piano strike certain keys whose letters spell a word and let the other members of the party guess what it is. If they can see the keyboard, and have been told in advance which keys represent the letters from A to G, it is by no means a difficult form of quiz even for the complete novice in music. Where the listeners are themselves really musical, it can be made harder by having the leader merely announce the key in which he is playing, or possibly the opening letter, and let them get the rest by ear. For those who are seriously learning their notes, this is wonderful practice.

For instance, the word CABBAGE makes an excellent short theme if played like this:

A slight change turns CABBAGE into BAGGAGE:

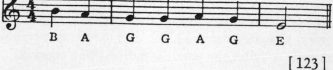

Here are some combinations of words easily spelled out on the keys of the piano:

If you wish to make the game a little harder, try building chords (or discords) which represent words if spelled from the bottom up or the top down. The following examples are fairly obvious:

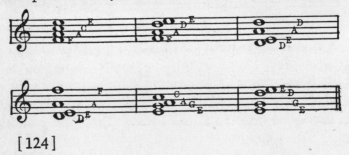

In Germany they have a habit of using the letter "H" for the note that we call B. (They apply the letter "B" to our B-flat.) This gives them a distinct advantage in forming words from notes, or melodies from words. They also call E-flat Es, which supplies them with the valuable letter "S." Thus Schumann was able to write charmingly in his *Carnaval* on the theme ASCH, which was the name of the home town of a girl with whom he was carrying on a flirtation—Ernestine von Fricken.

Franz Liszt wrote a *Fantasie and Fugue* on the letters of Bach's name, (Bach himself had worked a fugue out of the same four letters) and Schumann made a charming piano piece out of GADE, representing a contemporary fellow-composer—Niels Gade.

The reverse of the game suggested above is to give a good musician a word made up entirely of letters occurring in the musical alphabet and ask him to improvise a piece immediately on the letters. It is really not so difficult as it sounds, if done on a small scale. The blind pianist,

Alec Templeton, is a genius at such tricks and can produce an elaborate and beautiful composition on the spur of the moment, with only a few letters for a start. He will also combine three or more familiar melodies into a single piece of music, building it up with a wealth of technical skill.

A variation of "Musical Alphabet" substitutes numbers for letters. The absolute scale, from one note to its octave above, can be numbered from 1 to 8, with 9 and 10 added above if desired. House numbers of at least four digits, numbers on paper money or automobile licenses, and, of course, telephone numbers offer endless material for musical themes. Games can be played in the same way as with letters, either having the listeners guess what number a certain melody represents, or giving out numbers to a skilled pianist who turns them into complete compositions. This is another Templeton specialty and is also done effectively by Morton Gould, Geoffrey O'Hara, and other musicians. In fact, anyone with some ability to improvise can develop something interesting from almost any numerical combination, with the advantage of being permitted to put it into any key he prefers.

THE MUSICAL NUMBER GAME

If you think of the scale as numbered from one to eight (the eighth note being a duplication of the first, an octave higher), it is easy to work out a melody from any number of four or more digits. You can play in any key, for the relationship of the tones in the diatonic scale is always the same.

Generally it will be found easiest to use the key of C major, which has no sharps or flats. In that key the numbers from one to ten would represent the following notes:

C D E F G A B C D E
1 2 3 4 5 6 7 8 9 10

The number ten can be used to represent a cipher. It is not necessary to go beyond that, for an octave and a major third is about the limit of the average voice, and a good tune should not cover too great a range for singing.

HOW TO GET A NUMBER

Numbers can be secured in a variety of ways. If you are playing a game similar to "Musical Alphabet," let each one in the company select a number between one and ten. (It is best to limit the total to five or six numbers, as it is hard to remember more than this.) The one who is "it" can then be made to reproduce the numbers in tones at the piano or by whistling or humming or singing them. If "it" happens to be a good musician, there can be a demand that he or she make up a complete piece on the theme created by the numbers. The length of the notes and the basic rhythm can be left to the one who is making up the tune. In its simplest form, this game is merely a test of memory and the ability to form patterns, on the keys or in the musical mind, corresponding

[127]

to a series of numbers. But with real musicians playing, it may result in most interesting and attractive improvisations.

The license numbers on automobiles are good material for tunes constructed in this way. House numbers are all right if they contain as many as four digits (although even two or three notes will give you some kind of a start for a melody) and, of course, telephone numbers are ideal. Think of the start of *School Days* as 0595, and you will immediately see the possibilities of the trick.

A combination of letters and numbers can sometimes be used, as in a telephone number having two or more letters to be dialed in advance of the number. In New York, for instance, there might be such a number as Caledonia 5-3243. (There isn't really, otherwise it would be illegal to publish it here.) This number would be dialed as CA 5-3243, and in the key of C you could get from it an excellent tune of rather Russian flavor, which easily might be carried on further.

This was actually used in one of the radio programs, in the *Crime Clues* series, as a means of identifying a suspected criminal through some music he had written. A suggestion of the name of the suspect was also given musically through the following short theme, built from the nickname "Abe" and the initial "G":

A B E G   C A 5 3 2 4 3

(The name of the synthetic composition in the broadcast was *Concerto for Two Guns*.)

After telling an audience in Seattle about the fun of making up tunes from telephone numbers, etc., the author received an interesting letter from Marye Ellen Warner, which, with her permission, is here quoted in part. It is always gratifying to have one's ideas backed up in so practical a fashion, so take Mrs. Warner's word for it that it actually works:

> 922 South Third Street,
> Mount Vernon, Washington
>
> Dear Mr. Spaeth,
>
> When you lectured at the Athletic Club in Seattle last September and explained how much fun it was to set telephone numbers to music I became so enthusiastic about your idea that as soon as I got home I tried it out with the enclosed results. I've figured out a lot of telephone numbers and license plate numbers, but I've written only a few of them down. I played about six of them at the Ladies' Music Club during the "Music for Fun" program.
>
> People have become conscious of a humorous, clever side of music that they never dreamed existed. It's fun and they enjoy it! So do I! Since then I've played my telephone numbers for Rotary Clubs, Eastern Star meetings, D.A.R. meetings and Parent Teachers Association meetings.
>
> It's ever so much fun discovering music in numbers. You add a sharp here, a flat there, and the mood of the melody is instantly changed. Some numbers are more rhythmic than melodic. Some fit into "cut time" better than three-four or four-four time. It's ever so much fun walking down the street figuring out license plates. I've got an absolute sense of pitch so it's easy for me to hear the numbers as I see them.

When I improvised the numbers I played for the Music Club, I started out in the key of C. Rather, I used that as my "home base" like the pilots around Seattle use Boeing Field as their base. Once in the air, they fly anywhere and that's what I do once I establish my melodic idea. I can't remember if you did that, but I've found that it allows one more freedom to experiment. I detest unnecessary rules.

For the composition numbered 1341, a telephone number of a close friend of mine, I started in the key of C, using the note "C" as my starting point, but the result was unimpressive, like meat without salt, so I lowered the 2nd number 3 which was E, making it E-flat and immediately drifted into the key of A-flat. I played it for my cousin, who said the music suggested a beautiful spring day at Mt. Rainier. As she listened to the music, she seemed to be standing high on one of the slopes of the mountain gazing at the rugged beauty and grandeur of the snow-capped peaks. In the grass at her feet grew lush wild flowers. The sky was blue and sun shadows sparkled upon the branches of the evergreen trees. About and above her was beauty. Somehow I don't associate pictures or scenes with music. To me, it's melody and mood. 1341 suggested to me a sweet, lyrical mood, gay, with just a slight undercurrent of sadness and regret.

The number 621 was started in the key of C, too, rather I used that as my starting-point, but it sounded as if it were a part of the key of F, so that's where I ended it. The rhythmic pattern suggested triplets, which I used throughout the entire composition. Looking at the music in manuscript form, it appears monotonous, but I don't think it sounds that way. If I broke up the triplet idea and used a different rhythmic pattern in the middle of the piece, just for variety, that would break up the underlying beat of the piece, shatter the mood and destroy the illusion. So there wasn't anything else I could do but use the triplet idea once I had started it. I played it for a friend of mine, who said that it suggested to her a frightened child, lost, running through a forest, frequently glancing back in fear. The music suggested to her something far removed and remote from civilization.

Right now, married and isolated as I am in a small town, there is nothing for me to do but study band and orchestra under the High School director. It's fun (I play the sax and clarinet) and I'm learning a great deal, but sometimes I become very impatient.

There's an old Chinese proverb that says, "Every long journey begins with the first step," and I honestly believe that you pushed me on to my first step into something I as yet can't foresee. But something will come of it. Your clever suggestion has provided me with unlimited musical ideas. I could sit all day at the piano figuring out numbers. It's fascinating and I love it.

> Sincerely,
> MARYE ELLEN WARNER

FROM SPELLING TO READING

Through such games as these the fundamental grasp of the musical scale will inevitably be strengthened. Learning the names of the notes is a simple matter, and it is not difficult to remember how they look on the keyboard or on the engraved musical staff. But merely learning the letters, the keys, and the notes on the musical staff will not make you automatically a reader of music, any more than learning the English alphabet makes you a reader of books. Practice and experience are necessary before printed music becomes as simple and obvious as the printed word, and any diversion that adds to such experience is naturally helpful. The spelling bee of the rural school and radio has its parallel in musical spelling games, and both are of practical educational value, in addition to being most fascinating recreations.

After you have played "Musical Alphabet" enough times, the relationships of all the notes, from A to G, will become entirely familiar, and when the pattern of the diatonic scale is associated with the numbers 1 to 8, and these are identified in various familiar combinations, you may suddenly find that the whole theory of music, with the mathematics of melody and harmony, has become an open book in which you may in future read at will.

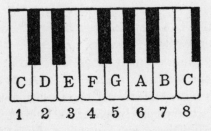

HOW MUSICAL ARE YOU ANYWAY?

If you want to test your basic musical ability in other ways than by attempting to grasp the meaning of notes and the progression of tones in the conventional scale, there are various records that have both a scientific background and a recreational significance. Such scholars as Carl Seashore and Jacob Kwalwasser have worked out elaborate tests whereby musical talent may be measured quite accurately in adults as well as children (a process that should be entirely unnecessary if parents took the advice of the strong-minded child quoted earlier in this book). Their approach can hardly be called recreational, and it is not recommended as material for a game.

But there is a simple phonograph record, prepared by the practical Joseph Maddy, which contains all the elements of amusing parlor competition. Dr. Maddy tests your sense of time and pitch and your feeling for harmony in such a painless fashion that you quite enjoy checking up with yourself, particularly as you are likely to get an excellent grade. There are one or two difficult spots in the record, but most of it is plain sailing and fairly sure to be flattering even to those who have very little musical ability.

This record can be used for testing those who are inclined to take music lessons, and it has the virtue of eliminating the obviously unfit and encouraging those who have the slightest chance of mastering an instrument. With the writer's cooperation a supplementary record has recently been prepared for testing the advancement of pupils after a certain number of lessons have been taken. Both records contain material for home competition and are supplied with printed blanks on which the answers can be written in the proper places and the final grades figured out. They can be as much fun as any of the intelligence games that have lately threatened the life of bridge and general conversation.*

Another game that can be played with phonograph records or with a good musician at the piano is the Musical Memory Test, which was popularized by C. M. Tremaine, director of the National Bureau for the

* These records are available at any Wurlitzer store.

Advancement of Music, and has been widely used in schools and homes, as well as for entire communities. The idea is simply to play excerpts from a number of compositions presumably familiar to the listeners. (The test can be based on a series of concerts, radio programs, or class studies previously covering a period of time, or merely selected from the recognized literature of music that everyone should know.) A system of grading can easily be worked out, with extra credit given to those who remember both the name of the piece and that of the composer.

For those who know something about music all kinds of refinements are possible in this memory game. They can be asked to give the key and perhaps the opus number of the composition in question, possibly even its date. They can even be quizzed on something comparatively unfamiliar, identifying the time signature (always fundamentally in two or three basic beats), possibly the key signature as well, certainly the major or minor mode, and perhaps a suggested title and the name of a credible composer. It is also fun, and by no means easy, to identify individual instruments in a phonograph record, but this game can be played only if there is an expert present to act as judge.

The Victor Company has made a series of records showing the tone color of all the orchestral instruments in short excerpts from actual compositions. These records make a fine test of the ear and memory, and they can be used by anyone, since the answers are all printed on the labels.

[134]

The success of intelligence tests and radio quizzes would seem to be founded on the combination of man's willingness to show off and the honest desire to gain more knowledge. Whatever the psychology may be, it has become clear that people of all ages today are glad to play games that require far more brains than did any of the common diversions of the past. If they are willing to work out *Crossword Puzzles*, *Ask Me Another*, *Twenty Questions*, *Who Am I?* and other brain teasers, there is reason to think that musical games requiring a little intelligence may also prove successful.

MUSICAL QUIZZES FOR ALL

Radio programs such as the *Symphonic Varieties* and *Kay Kyser's Musical Kollege* have emphasized the fact that people are interested in questions concerning music, both serious and popular. Most of the quiz books contain some musical material (the *Giant Quiz Book* devotes a whole section to music) and there is now a vastly entertaining and informative book called *The Music Quiz*, by Gladys Burch and Helmut Ripperger (Stackpole Sons), which will keep any group of musically minded people busy for hours at a time.

Games to a musical accompaniment are, of course, common—from *Going to Jerusalem* to a Virginia reel or elaborate folk-dances, and there is no need to dwell here upon the possibilities of such fun with music. Ballroom dancing is in itself a game of eternal popularity, and there is encouragement in the modern tendency to take up again the rather complicated figures and evolutions

[135]

once associated with quadrilles, lancers, and cotillions, but now disguised as the *Big Apple*, the *Lambeth Walk*, and what not. Willingness to take part in a "square dance" is always a sign of the communal, cooperative party spirit, a welcome relief from the mere sexercise of the waltz and the fox-trot.

YOU TOO CAN DANCE

Dancing, at best or worst, always contains the elements of popular recreation, and even amateurs have definitely developed it as an art. One sees beautiful interpretations of the tango, for instance, on almost any dance floor, and you do not have to be a professional to give an expert performance of the rumba, the shag, the Susie-Q, or even a complicated tap dance—perhaps the best exercise of all. Out in Hawaii the native teachers actually make excellent hula dancers out of the visiting white girls from the mainland, and the Hawaiians, of all people, know how to get the greatest possible recreational value from their music.

Participation is the final answer to the true enjoyment of any art. Music offers to practically everyone the possibility of singing and dancing. But it reserves some special joys for those who are willing and able to play together in instrumental groups, from simple duets up to creditable amateur orchestras.*

* Two books that present this rather specialized enjoyment of music in irresistible fashion are Catherine Drinker Bowen's *Friends and Fiddlers* (Little, Brown & Co.) and *A Little Night Music*, by Gerald Johnson (Harper & Brothers).

[136]

That great pianist, Harold Bauer, has devoted much time and thought to the encouragement of small groups of amateur musicians in ensemble playing. Its possibilities are appreciated only by those who have tried it. The joy of picking up an entrance correctly, of hearing yourself as part of an effect that you could never produce alone, most of all of getting right into the heart and soul of a composer by trying to play what he wrote—that is something indescribable and, to too many people, incomprehensible. An instrumental combination of any sort, representing a family, a club, or even a haphazard group of neighbors, beats any musical game ever invented. Why not participate?

BIBLIOGRAPHY AND NOTES

In addition to the books and other helps already noted in the preceding chapter, the following are worth mentioning for their general cooperation with the game of music: *Creative School Music*, by Lillian Fox and L. Thomas Hopkins (Silver, Burdett & Co.); *Treasure Bag of Game Songs*, by Dorothy Gordon (E. P. Dutton & Co.); *Sing, Swing, Play*, by Martha Stockton Russell (Viking Press); and *The Magic of Music*, Robert H. Schauffler (Dodd, Mead & Co.). Various card games and other devices are on the market, ready made for musical recreation of a flexible type. The card games include *The Great Composers* (Theodore Presser & Co.); the *Dewhirst Music Game* (Cora Grace Dewhirst); *Musicards* (Bruce Humphries); *Self-Instruction Music Cards* (Dulcet Conservatory); and Leonard Adams' packs entitled *Rhythm* and *Analogues* (Notation). There are also *Musical Dominoes* and *Musical Lotto*.

A LISTENER'S LIBRARY

To GET the most fun out of music it is almost necessary to take part in it, even in a very modest fashion. Singing in a crowd is at least something, if an actual instrument is out of reach.

But there is enormous pleasure to be found also in the mere process of listening, with all the possibilities of records; the radio; school, club, church, and theater music; and eventually the concert hall and opera house. Unless the music heard is of the type that has no lasting quality, familiarity breeds enjoyment, not contempt.

There is a particular excitement in discovering a piece of music that grows more fascinating with each successive hearing—particularly if each time the listener finds new beauties that he had not suspected before. This is the real explanation of the attitude of the confirmed concertgoer, and it may explain also why so many people would rather hear something that they already know than to experiment with unfamiliar material, no matter how good.

Of course there must be a first time for everything, and the listener is fortunate if a new piece is introduced in the presence of someone who has heard it before and can therefore build a proper predisposition to enthusiasm. It always helps to be placed in a receptive mood, and if the novelty then turns out to be honestly enjoyable, the pleasure is all the greater.

Every great composition can stand practically unlimited repetition, following the well-known law of the survival of the fittest. Whatever is cheap and obvious and commonplace, even though it may exert an immediate appeal, fails when put to the test of permanence.

POPULAR SONGS HAVE THEIR TROUBLES

The average popular song is a good example. Its very nature demands that it be quickly and easily remembered. By the time radio has done its work, reminding you of the same hackneyed tune ten or a dozen times a day, the life of that tune is doomed. Six months is about the limit of its activity, and six weeks will often suffice to kill it completely.

The average listener makes these decisions himself, showing thereby a fundamental appreciation of the things that are not transient but permanent.

But how shall the person totally inexperienced in music discover for himself the things that are permanent? Unfortunately, if he is exposed to them without preparation or a preliminary build-up, they are likely to sound very dull, and the enthusiasm of a confirmed music-lover is merely wasted. The novice may honestly admire the perfection of Toscanini's performance of an abstruse work, but that does not mean that he will remember or in the slightest degree appreciate the work itself.

Try to interest such a person directly in a Bach fugue, a Beethoven sonata, a Brahms symphony or a Wagner opera, regardless of interpretation, and see how much progress you will make. It simply cannot be done. The people who love and appreciate those great classics today forget that they first went through various stages of enjoying lighter pieces, including perhaps some down-right trash. They listened to plenty of bad music and some that was only fairly good, and they gradually eliminated from their listening repertoire everything that did not pass the test of time—at least, as far as they were concerned.*

This matter of permanence in music presents curious problems. The giddy, scatterbrained jitterbug is ready to accept any hot record by a popular dance band as the last word in significant music. At the other extreme, the ultramodernist is no longer sure that the accepted classics of the "three B's" are really the climax of absolute music or that Wagner and Richard Strauss went as far as possible on the dramatic side.

* An interesting book has recently been published, called *A Music Album*, built on the basic idea of a stamp album. Composers take the place of countries, and a stamp is pasted in each time the owner first hears a particular piece by that composer. The compiler is Samuel G. Houghton (William Morrow & Co., Inc.).

Permanence seems to be a relative term after all, except insofar as it represents practically a unanimity of opinion over a considerable period of time. But one man's permanence in music may be another man's passing fancy.

The person who has become engrossed in the pursuit of music, either as a listener or as a performer, will not be satisfied with compositions which to the dilettante or the frankly unmusical observer may seem the ultimate in musical beauty. A great many listeners, obviously, have never gone beyond the platitudes and clichés of popular music. Some have stopped at Grieg, Macdowell, Nevin, Chaminade, perhaps Dvorak. To still others, permanence represents the lighter works of the greatest masters, and beyond this there is still the bulk of the real music-lovers, the hide-bound classicists, the modernists, and the ultramodernists.

BRING ON THE EXECUTIONERS

Now, here is a heretical thought, which is uttered deliberately and in all sincerity. Take it for what it is worth and let it cure your inferiority complex if possible. *You can have just as much fun with the music of Grieg and Nevin and Chaminade as a highbrow has with that of Bach and Beethoven and Brahms.* Actually, you may enjoy it even more, for your pleasure will be direct and natural, unhampered by intellectual considerations.

There are only certain people who have the time, the inclination, and the innate gifts to develop a sincere

[141]

enjoyment of music that to the average listener sounds extremely complicated, hopelessly difficult, and perhaps downright dull. It would be absurd to try to bring everybody up to that level of intelligent appreciation, even though it may be entirely possible for anyone willing to make the effort.

The point is that anybody honestly enjoying any kind of music, from a popular song to a classic symphony, is going through somewhat the same process—part physical (the response to rhythm), part emotional (the response to melody, harmony, and tone color), part intellectual (the response to form and technique). The fundamental stimuli may be quite different, but the sensations of pleasure are likely to possess a definite similarity.

WHAT IS MUSICAL ENJOYMENT?

The pleasure derived from music is at best not accurately definable. You yourself are the only one who knows if you have it, and so long as you are satisfied, that is all that really matters. It is far better to feel the thrill of honestly enjoying some comparatively insignificant music than to pretend to like something that secretly bores you to death.

If you like the music of some of the minor composers and keep on listening, the chances are that you will eventually discover the major ones also and possibly develop for them the same sincere enjoyment. To help the listener in this quest of permanent music, a progressive library is suggested below. Take it or leave it, as a whole or in part. You may not need any suggestions at all along this line.

Unfortunately, radio has hammered away at the so-called "light classics" with such grim determination that many of them have now become as dead as last year's popular song. This is a pity, for most of these little pieces have a distinct charm and are decidedly useful for creating an interest in music if they are not played to death. There is a great deal of music, not even mentioned here, which is played in those early morning broadcasts that give commuters the time for making their trains. Most of it is negligible, and the list below is limited to music that is at least attached to a fairly well-known name, and in many cases a name that represents truly great music that may be discovered later. The surprising thing is that all of the great names appear at least once among even the most obviously enjoyable pieces.

The material in general is available on phonograph records and is likely to be heard on the radio and in the concert hall and opera house.

The list applies equally to young and old; and, by the way, its first two groups represent in fairly good music exactly those qualities of rhythm and melody that make for the success of popular music. The persistent pursuer of music can always find something among the "light classics" that will offer the same appeal of syncopation, smoothly flowing melody, interesting harmony, or exciting instrumentation as the most appealing of current popular numbers. So here is a listener's library of sure-fire material, progressively arranged, from the fairly obvious, easily enjoyed pieces, up through various degrees of difficulty, to the great masterpieces themselves, but with nothing completely beyond the grasp of the average ear.

I. VERY EASY ON THE EAR

(These are all short pieces. Nothing long is really easy on the ear of the novice.)

Arensky—*Waltz for Two Pianos.*
Bach—*Gavotte, Bourrée, Loure, Gigue, Sarabande,* etc.
Beethoven—*Minuet in G, Country Dances, Turkish March,* and *Chorus of Dervishes* from *The Ruins of Athens.*
Berlioz—*Dance of the Sylphs, Rakoczy March.*
Boccherini—*Minuet.*
Brahms—*Lullaby, The Little Sandman, Hungarian Dances, Waltzes.*
Chaminade—*Scarf Dance, The Flatterer, Pas des Amphores.*
Chopin—*Butterfly Étude; Black Key Étude; Prelude No. 6 in B minor, No. 7 in A major, No. 20 in C minor; Nocturne No. 2 in E-flat; Waltz No. 6 in D-flat, No. 7 in C-sharp minor, No. 11 in G-flat, No. 14 in E minor.*
Czibulcka—*La Czarina Mazurka.*
Debussy—*Arabesque, Rêverie, Golliwog's Cakewalk,* and *The Little Shepherd* from *Children's Corner.*
Delibes—Ballet music from *Coppelia, Sylvia,* etc.
Dett, R. Nathaniel—*Juba Dance.*
Dvorak—*Humoresque, Slavonic Dances.*

Elgar—*Salut d' Amour, Pomp and Circumstance March.*

Fibich—*Poème* (used as melody of *My Moonlight Madonna*).

Folk-music—*The Arkansas Traveler, Turkey in the Straw, Irish Washerwoman, Londonderry Air, Kol Nidrei, Negro Spirituals, Volga Boat Song,* Folk-songs of various nations.

Gardner, Samuel—*From the Cane Brake.*

German, Edward—Dances from *Henry VIII.*

Gershwin—*Rhapsody in Blue.*

Godard—*Berceuse* from *Jocelyn.*

Gounod—*Ave Maria, Funeral March of a Marionette,* Ballet music and *Soldier's Chorus* from *Faust.*

Grainger—*Country Gardens, Shepherd's Hey, Molly on the Shore, Mock Morris.*

Grieg—*Peer Gynt Suite,* especially *Morning, Anitra's Dance,* and *In the Hall of the Mountain King, Last Spring, Heart Wounds, Erotikon, To Spring, I Love You, Norwegian Bridal Procession.*

Handel—*Largo, The Harmonious Blacksmith.*

Haydn—*Toy Symphony,* Slow movement of *Surprise Symphony, Gypsy Rondo* from *Trio.*

Herbert—*Al Fresco, American Fantasy, Babillage.*

Humperdinck—*Prayer* and *Dream Music* from *Hänsel and Gretel.*

Järnefeldt—*Prelude* and *Berceuse.*

Kreisler—*Caprice Viennois, Liebesfreud, Liebesleid, Schön Rosmarin, Tambourin Chinois.*

Liadow—*Music Box.*

Liszt—*Liebestraum, Hungarian Rhapsody, No. 2, Gnomenreigen, Waldesrauschen.*

MacDowell—*To a Wild Rose, To a Water Lily, A.D. 1620, Scotch Poem, Witches' Dance.*

Mascagni—*Intermezzo* from *Cavalleria Rusticana.*

Massenet—*Meditation* from *Thaïs, Élégie.*

Mendelssohn—*Spring Song, Rondo Capriccioso, Overture* and *Wedding March* from *A Midsummer Night's Dream, On Wings of Song.*

Moszkowski—*Serenade, Spanish Dance.*

Mozart—*Lullaby,* almost any of the *Minuets.*

Nevin—*Narcissus, A Day in Venice, The Rosary.*

Offenbach—*Barcarolle* from *Tales of Hoffman.*

Paderewski—*Minuet.*

Ponchielli—*Dance of the Hours* from *La Gioconda.*

Powell, John—*The Banjo Picker.*

Rachmaninoff—*Preludes in C-sharp minor* and *G minor.*

Rimsky-Korsakoff—*Song of India, Flight of the Bumblebee.*

Rubinstein—*Melody in F, Kamenoi-Ostrow.*

Saint-Saëns—*The Swan, Danse Macabre.*

Schubert—*Serenade, Ave Maria, Moment Musical, Military March, Waltzes.*

Schumann—*Träumerei, The Happy Farmer,* and other *Scenes from Childhood.*

Scott, Cyril—*Lullaby, Negro Dance.*

Sibelius—*Valse Triste, Finlandia.*

Strauss, Johann, Jr.—*Waltzes,* including *The Beautiful Blue Danube, Roses from the South, Tales from the Vienna Woods, Vienna Blood, Artists' Life,* and *Voices of Spring.*

Strauss, Richard—Waltzes from *Der Rosenkavalier.*

Tschaikowsky—*Nutcracker Suite, Song without Words, Humoresque, Troika, Marche Slav, June Barcarolle.*

Verdi—*Triumphal March* from *Aida,* Anvil Chorus from *Il Trovatore.*

Wagner—*March, Pilgrims' Chorus,* and *Song to the Evening Star* from *Tannhäuser; Wedding March* from *Lohengrin; Prize Song* from *Die Meistersinger; Ride of the Valkyries* and *Magic Fire Music* from *Die Walküre.*

Weber—*Invitation to the Dance.*

II. FAIRLY EASY ON THE EAR

Bach—*Air on the G String, Prelude in C major, Arioso, Invention in F major, Jesu, Joy of Man's Desiring.*

Beethoven—Overtures: *Egmont, Coriolanus, Leonore, No. 3;* Slow movements of most of the symphonies and sonatas.

Bizet—Nearly all of *Carmen,* especially the *Overture, Habanera, Seguidilla, Toreador Song,* Ballet music, and *Interludes; Suite* from *l'Arlésienne.*

Borodin—Dances from *Prince Igor.*

Brahms—*Academic Festival Overture,* Various short piano pieces.

Chabrier—*Espana Rhapsody.*

Chopin—*Prelude No. 15 in B-flat, No. 17 in A-flat,* and *No. 23 in F; Revolutionary Étude; Fantasie Impromptu in C-sharp minor; Military Polonaise* and *Polonaise in A-flat; Impromptu in F-sharp; Barcarolle;* various *Mazurkas; Waltz No. 2 in A-flat, No. 3 in A minor,*

No. 5 in A-flat, No. 10 in B minor, and No. 12 in F minor; Funeral March; Nocturnes.

Debussy—*Clair de Lune,Festivals.*

Donizetti—*Sextet* from *Lucia di Lammermoor.*

Dvorak—*Largo* from *New World Symphony* (also known as *Goin' Home*), *Carnival Overture.*

Enesco—*Roumanian Rhapsody.*

Gershwin—*An American in Paris.*

Glazounoff—*Ballet of the Seasons*, especially *Autumn.*

Glinka—*Overture* to *Russlan and Ludmilla.*

Gluck—*Gavotte, Elysian Fields Music* from *Orpheus and Eurydice.*

Goldmark—*Sakuntala Overture.*

Grieg—Songs, such as *Im Kahne, A Swan, Solveig's Song,* etc.; *Romance* from *String Quartet;* Short piano pieces, such as *Papillon (Butterfly)* and *Berceuse.*

Hadley—*Ballet of the Flowers, Angelus.*

Handel—*Where'er You Walk, Hallelujah Chorus* from *The Messiah.*

Haydn—*Variations* from *Emperor Quartet; Surprise, Clock,* and *Military* symphonies.

Ippolitoff-Ivanoff—*Caucasian Sketches, March of the Sirdar.*

Kreisler—Imitations of old violin music and arrangements of short classics.

Leoncavallo—Excerpts from *Pagliacci*—especially the *Prologue, Ballatella,* and *Harlequin's Serenade.*

Liszt—*La Campanella; Hungarian Rhapsodies, No. 1, No. 6,* and *No. 12; Hungarian Fantasy.*

MacDowell—*Indian Suite, Polonaise,* songs—including *The Sea* and *Thy Beaming Eyes.*

Massenet—Excerpts from *Manon,* including the *Gavotte.*

Meyerbeer—*Coronation March* from *The Prophet.*

Mendelssohn—*Fingal's Cave Overture, Songs without Words,* Trio *Lift Thine Eyes, Scherzo* from *A Midsummer Night's Dream, Priests' March* from *Athalia.*

Mozart—*Alleluja,* Operatic Overtures.

Nicolai—*Overture* to *The Merry Wives of Windsor.*

Puccini—*One Fine Day* and other excerpts from *Madame Butterfly, Musetta's Song* and arias of Rodolpho and Mimi from *La Bohême.*

Ravel—*Bolero, Pavane for a Dead Infanta, Sonatine.*

Rimsky-Korsakoff—*Spanish Caprice.*

Rossini—*Overture* and ballet music from *William Tell, Overture* and excerpts from *The Barber of Seville, Overture* to *Semiramide.*

Saint-Saëns—*Habanera, Rondo Capriccioso, Carnival of the Animals, Phaeton.*

Schubert—Ballet music from *Rosamunde, Impromptus, Unfinished Symphony,* Songs—including *The Erlking, Who is Sylvia?* and *Hark, Hark the Lark.*

Schumann—*The Prophet Bird; Warum?; Papillons;* Songs like *The Two Grenadiers, The Lotus Flower,* and *Du bist wie eine Blume.*

Smetana—*Overture* to *The Bartered Bride,* and Dances.

Strauss, Johann, Jr.—*Overture* to *Die Fledermaus (The Bat)* and any waltzes not yet heard.

Sullivan—Practically all the operettas written with Gilbert.

Thomas—*Gavotte* and other selections from *Mignon.*

Tschaikowsky—*Overture 1812, Italian Caprice,* Waltzes from *Eugen Onegin, Andante Cantabile* from *String Quartet.*

Verdi—*Quartet* and other selections from *Rigoletto,* excerpts from *Aïda, Ballo in Maschera, Forza del Destino,* and *Il Trovatore.*

Wagner—*Siegfried Idyl; Overtures* to *The Flying Dutchman, Rienzi,* and *Tannhäuser; Prelude* to *Die Meistersinger; Prelude* and special *Prelude to Act III* of *Lohengrin.*

Weber—*Overtures* to *Oberon* and *Der Freischütz.*

Weinberger—*Polka* and *Fugue* from *Schwanda the Bagpiper.*

Wieniawski—*Souvenir de Moscow.*

Wolf-Ferrari—*Intermezzo* from *The Jewels of the Madonna.*

III. A BIT DEMANDING ON THE EAR

Albeniz—*Iberia, Triana, Seguidilla.*

Bach—*Preludes* and *Fugues* from *The Well-tempered Clavichord, Choral Preludes, French* and *English Suites.*

Beethoven—*Symphonies,* 2, 6, 7, and 8, preferably in that order; *Moonlight Sonata.*

Berlioz—*Roman Carnival Overture, Benvenuto Cellini.*

Brahms—*Songs, Tragic Overture, Serenades for Orchestra, Quintet, Edward Ballade, Liebeslieder Waltzes, Zigeunerlieder.*

Carpenter, J. A.—*Adventures in a Perambulator, Krazy Kat Ballet, Skyscrapers.*

Charpentier—Selections from *Louise.*

Chopin—*Ballades, Scherzos.*

Debussy—*Afternoon of a Faun, Clouds, Iberia,* Piano pieces, Songs.

Dukas—*The Sorcerer's Apprentice.*

Dvorak—*New World Symphony* (entire).

Gershwin—*Piano Concerto in F, Porgy and Bess.*

Granados—*Spanish Dances.*

Grieg—*Piano Concerto, Violin Sonatas,* Songs.

Hadley—*Overture In Bohemia.*

Handel—*Water Music, Concerti Grossi.*

Haydn—*London Symphonies, Cello Concerto.*

Lalo—*Symphonie Espagnole.*

Liszt—*Les Préludes, Mephisto Waltz, Faust Symphony, Piano Concertos in E-flat* and *A major, Études, Tasso.*

MacDowell —*Piano Concerto in D minor.*

Mendelssohn—*Violin Concerto,* Chamber music.

Moussorgsky—*A Night on Bald Mountain.*

Mozart—*Piano* and *Violin Concertos* and *Sonatas,* Selections from *The Magic Flute.*

Powell, John—*Negro Rhapsody.*

Prokofieff—*March* from *The Love of Three Oranges.*

Puccini—Excerpts from *La Tosca.*

Ravel—*Jeux d'eau, Mother Goose.*

Respighi—*Fountains of Rome, Pines of Rome, Roman Festivals.*

Rimsky-Korsakoff—*Scheherazade, Le Coq d'Or.*

Schelling—*A Victory Ball*.

Saint-Saëns—Excerpts from *Samson and Delila*, *Piano Concerto No. 2*.

Schubert—*Quartet in D minor* (*Death and the Maiden*), *Piano Quintet in A major* (*The Trout*), Songs.

Schumann—*Symphonic Études*, *Carnaval*, *Sonata in F minor*.

Sibelius—*The Swan of Tuonela*, *En Saga*.

Strauss, Richard—Songs—especially *Allerseelen*, *Morgen*, *Traum durch die Dämmerung*, *Zueignung*.

Stravinsky—*Fireworks*, *Petrouschka*.

Taylor, Deems—*Through the Looking Glass Suite*.

Tschaikowsky—*Romeo and Juliet Overture*, *Francesca da Rimini*, *Piano Concerto in B-flat minor*, *Violin Concerto in D major*.

Verdi—Excerpts from *Otello*, *Falstaff*, *Manzoni Requiem*.

Wagner—*Träume*, *Prelude* to *Tristan und Isolde*, *Prelude* to *Parsifal*, Excerpts from *Tannhäuser* and *Lohengrin*.

Weber—*Overture* to *Euryanthe*.

IV. THE REAL THING

Bach—*Brandenburg Concertos*, *Cantatas*, *Chaconne*, *Passacaglia*, *St. Matthew Passion*, *Mass in B minor*.

Beethoven—*Symphonies*, *Nos. 3, 5, and 9; Violin Concerto; Piano Concertos in C minor*, *G major*, and *E-flat* (*Emperor*); *Kreutzer Sonata* for violin; *Pathétique* and *Appassionata Sonatas* for piano; *Fidelio*.

Berlioz—*Damnation of Faust*, *Romeo and Juliet Symphony*, *Requiem*.

Brahms—*Symphonies, Nos. 1, 2, 3,* and *4; Violin Concerto; Piano Concertos, Nos. 1 and 2.*

Chopin—*Sonatas, Piano Concertos in E minor* and *F minor, Fantasie in F minor.*

Debussy—*La Mer, Pelléas et Mélisande, String Quartet.*

Franck, César—*Symphony in D minor, Violin Sonata, Chorale, Fantasie,* and *Fugue.*

Handel—*The Messiah.*

Haydn—*The Creation.*

Mendelssohn—*Elijah, Italian Symphony, Scotch Symphony.*

Moussorgsky—*Boris Godounoff.*

Mozart—*Jupiter Symphony, Symphonies in E-flat* and *G minor,* Selections from *Don Giovanni* and *Figaro.*

Ravel—*La Valse, Daphnis et Chloe, String Quartet.*

Schubert—*Symphony in C major.*

Schumann—*Symphonies, No. 1, No. 2, No. 3,* and *No. 4; Piano Concerto in A minor.*

Sibelius—*Symphonies, No. 1, No. 2, No. 4,* and *No. 5.*

Strauss, Richard—*Death and Transfiguration, Don Juan, Till Eulenspiegel, A Hero's Life.*

Stravinsky—*The Firebird, Rites of Spring.*

Tschaikowsky—*Symphonies, No. 4, No. 5,* and *No. 6 (Pathétique).*

Wagner—*Das Rheingold, Die Walküre, Siegfried, Götterdämmerung, Die Meistersinger, Tristan und Isolde, Parsifal.*

Once you have heard most of the music in the last group, you can decide for yourself how far you want to go in the direction of ultramodernism, or to what extent you want to dig up the more obscure masterpieces, always a fascinating game with musical scholars. Actually, you could spend the rest of your life digesting the materials of just this final group.

If you never get that far, there is plenty of great music in the third group, and plenty of enjoyment to be found in the first and second. Besides, there is also a considerable amount of popular music that belongs in the class of these first two groups and possibly higher. The dividing line is becoming less distinct every year, and again permanence is the only answer.

CLASSICS ARE POPULAR MUSIC

A so-called "classic" is really more popular than any current success, judged by the total number of hearings it has had; and a piece that starts with immediate popularity may show such lasting value that it becomes automatically a classic in time. Don't forget that the Foster songs were the popular music of their day. They happened to possess a vitality and a peculiar type of inspiration that made them permanent.

The Long, Long Trail, which became popular during the World War, has already proved its permanence and may be considered a classic of its kind today. *Old Man River* seems on its way to similar immortality.

The light operas and musical comedies of Victor Herbert, George Gershwin, Jerome Kern, Romberg, Lehar, Friml, and other composers have a quality of

[154]

permanence similar to that of the Gilbert and Sullivan masterpieces and the eternally popular Strauss waltzes, and should be recognized as excellent music. Irving Berlin, Cole Porter, Arthur Schwartz, Richard Rodgers, Vincent Youmans, and Hoagey Carmichael are only a few of the popular composers whose songs generally have a definite musical value, and all of them have produced numbers that have a chance to achieve the "classic" label and are already accepted as "standard" (by which a popular publisher means almost anything lasting more than a year or two).

OUR NATIVE PRODUCT

America's own music of the future is likely to be a combination of serious forms with popular idioms, as already used successfully by Gershwin, Grofé, and a few others, with radio and the screen as its most practical media. That should be encouraging to anyone who still finds it hard to get beyond the obvious rhythms and melodies of Tin-Pan Alley. These may be considered "city folk-music," as contrasted with the rural folk-music that is recognized all over the world. At their best, such materials may be picked up and developed into serious masterpieces, exactly as most of the great composers at some time deliberately borrowed and elaborated the actual folk-tunes of their own countries.

It is not really necessary to draw a dividing line between the "popular" and the "classic," and those who

[155]

have heard enough music of all kinds quickly get rid of the habit. Listening is fun in any case, as long as it is not a mere pose or the performance of a duty. Don't try to analyze your reactions, and don't worry about your musical taste or the sneers of the highbrows. You are getting fun out of music. That is the main thing.

IDENTIFYING THE COMPOSERS

T HERE are some people who like to do nothing but *talk* about music. They do not make any attempt to take part in it, and when they go to a concert or the opera they are altogether likely to sit in a comfortable coma or luscious lethargy and not really listen at all. But they are full of fine-sounding phrases that have a very learned air, and they can pronounce all the names correctly and perhaps tell you a lot of musical history and biography, including opus numbers and key signatures. Ask them to identify a tune and they are usually stuck.

It is not very difficult to become a music-lover of that sort. To make it still easier, here are a few facts and figures which are not hard to remember, and with them the sort of talk that will always make an impression on the uninitiated. It means nothing, of course. But it is harmless.

You already have in the preceding chapter a list of the outstanding works by the great composers and also those pieces that you are most likely to hear. Being able to place them geographically and historically will do no harm, and it may actually increase your desire to hear the music, which is far more important. You can always look up dates and other facts in a dictionary. But if you have heard enough of a composer's work to be able to say with some conviction, "That is by So-and-So," even though you have not heard it before, it means you are becoming a pretty good music-lover. It is also gratifying to express a favorable opinion of some composition that is new to you and then find that it is by a recognized composer. The talk-specialists are likely to ask "Who wrote it?" before venturing an opinion.

With this handy little guide, you will be able to talk back at the people who know all the answers, and if after a while you can insert an original idea of your own, that will be wonderful. There are far too many labels and formulas and traditions and rules in music as it is. The people who attract attention are the ones who upset them, not the stodgy conformers.

A GUIDE TO THE MASTERS

Johann Sebastian Bach. German. B. Eisenach, 1685; d. Leipzig, 1750. "The Father of Modern Music." A hardworking organist and choirmaster all his life. Father of twenty children, several of whom became famous musicians. Perhaps the greatest musical technician of all time, but also an inspired creator of melodies, full of human qualities and dramatic power. "His polyphonic effects are so wonderful." "What a pity he did not write an opera!" "If you can play Bach, you can play anything." "If the old man once gets you, he'll never let you go." "What a dynamo of work and inspiration!"

Ludwig van Beethoven. German. B. Bonn, 1770; d. Vienna, 1827. "The Colossus." Small in size, but a giant in music, he upset many of the existing ideas and laid the foundation for the whole romantic movement, substituting human emotion for formal beauty. Considered a rebel and a heretic in his day, he is now ranked at the top, with only Bach, Brahms, and Wagner to rival him. His symphonies, concertos, sonatas, and chamber music are definitely among the greatest. "Isn't it amazing that a deaf man could write such music!" "That sturdy independence that is Beethoven!" "Nobody else ever wrote such slow themes." "I'm sure he was a great genius, but I'd hate to have to live with him."

Johannes Brahms. German. B. Hamburg, 1833; d. Vienna, 1897. "Third of the three B's." Also a short, stocky man, combining the best features of classicism and romanticism. He wrote symphonies, concertos, sonatas, and chamber music of technical perfection but great human appeal, and was also one of the greatest of song writers. His temperament showed only in his music. "He never married and he never wrote an opera." "You get a feeling of ineffable calm." "It takes several hearings before you begin to realize the beauty of his workmanship." "The musicians' musician." "Strange that anyone should ever have thought Brahms abstruse and dull." "Absolute music at its highest peak."

[159]

Frederic Chopin (pronounced Show-pan). Polish. B. near Warsaw, 1810; d. Paris, 1849. "The Poet of the Piano." A frail and sickly genius, who did far more than write perfect piano music. His ideas are the basis of the whole modern school, and his music holds its own even in comparison with the great orchestral works. Even an exercise became personal and human in his hands, and the virility of his work belies the suggestion of effeminacy given by his pictures. "He decorates a melody with all the elaborations of Gothic architecture." "Chopin alone knew how to make the piano *sing*." "If only he had not been dominated by that masterful woman, George Sand!" "I always say if a pianist can play Chopin, he can play anything." "Too bad he died so young. He might have written an opera!"

Claude Achille Debussy (pronounced Deh-bü-see, with the accents evenly distributed). French. B. near Paris, 1862; d. Paris, 1918. "Music's Great Impressionist." The real founder of the modern school and first to make general use of harmonies and tone colors now universally accepted. Composing mostly in the smaller forms, for the piano and the voice, he also wrote several highly significant orchestral works and one unique opera, *Pelléas et Melisande*. His method of fusing tones together created a subtle background of color that was entirely new to music. "You can always tell Debussy by his harmonies." "His music sounds so *French*, if you know what I mean." "Just to think that only a few years ago we thought all that was frightfully revolutionary and rather ugly too. Time marches on." "A piece by Debussy always makes me think of a painting by Monet, or is it Manet?"

César Franck. Belgian. B. Liège, 1822; d. Paris, 1890. "The Organist of Ste. Clothilde." A modern edition of Bach, he combined great scholarship with peculiarly winning qualities as a human being. Modest and retiring, he scarcely let the world know of his creative work. He wrote only one symphony, but it has placed him among the most popular composers in that field. "I always say my favorite symphony is César Franck's. It's so nice not to have to tell which one." "Such a lovely old man! He said it sounded exactly the way he thought it would." "The themes never seem to end. They keep going forever." "Now I know where the tune of *Masquerade* came from."

George Frederick Handel. German. B. Halle, 1685; d. London, 1759. "Master of Oratorio." Remembered today almost entirely by *The Messiah* and one little melody (the *Largo*), but actually very prolific and successful. Forty operas are completely forgotten, except for occasional excerpts, and more than twenty-five oratorios and cantatas have shared the same fate. Handel's music is remarkable for the breadth of the melodic line, which he sustains in a manner consistently equaled by no other composer. His part-writing for voices is also full of inspiration. *The Messiah* alone would make him immortal "I always wonder if he took off that big wig when he started to compose." "You can pronounce him just like *handle*, because when he went to England he anglicized his name. I'd rather think of him as English anyway." "The broad Handelian phrase —when shall we see its like again?" "Funny that Handel and Bach should have been born in the same year but never met throughout their lives. They both went blind, too, before they died." "I like *The Messiah* because it always makes me think of Christmas shopping."

Franz Joseph Haydn (pronounced Hide'n). Austrian. B. Rohrau, 1732; d. Vienna, 1809. "Father of the Symphony." Affectionately known also as "Papa" Haydn, this composer is a well-loved figure in the history of music. He was supported by the Esterhazy princes and later by the London public in such a way that he had plenty of time to write quantities of good music, and he unquestionably deserves credit for first working out the principles of sonata form in general and the symphony in particular. He wrote over a hundred symphonies altogether, besides much chamber music, concertos, oratorios, and songs. He represents the classic model of form. "Papa Haydn always had to have his little joke." "What a wonderful disposition for a henpecked husband!" "I like that story about getting a Christmas vacation for the orchestra by writing his *Farewell Symphony* and letting them gradually blow out all the candles." "There is more to Haydn than his jokes and his disposition. Toscanini makes him sound really significant."

[162]

Franz Liszt. Hungarian. B. Raiding, 1811; d. Bayreuth, 1886. "The Giant of the Keyboard." Recognized as the most sensational pianist of all time, Liszt gets far less credit as a composer. His chief claim to fame is that he invented the Symphonic Poem, but his popularity rests mostly on his *Hungarian Rhapsodies* (built on folk-tunes) and the sentimental *Liebestraum*. Wagner, who married his daughter Cosima, unquestionably got many of his melodic ideas from Liszt. "He was very generous to other composers, and that is a rare trait." "I prefer to think of Liszt as the Great Lover. It makes him so human." "What a pity that long hair has gone out of style for pianists!" "I once knew a pianist who studied with a pupil of Liszt." "Even if you don't take him seriously as a composer, he was an Artistic and Intellectual Force."

Felix Mendelssohn (Bartholdy). German. B. Hamburg, 1809; d. Leipzig, 1847. "The Lucky Boy." One of the few composers to grow up in comfortable circumstances, son of a banker and grandson of a famous philosopher. A child prodigy, so gifted that his facility often blinded people to the value of his work. Definitely of the romantic school, he revered the classics and was largely responsible for the revival of Bach. His love of melody and refusal to create sensational effects for their own sake have brought him belittlement by those who could not imitate his pure style. "Think of a boy of seventeen writing the *Overture* to the *Midsummer Night's Dream*.

I thought Max Reinhardt did a lot with it." "You can talk about *The Messiah*, but give me Mendelssohn's *Elijah* for drama *and* religion." "Those lovely *Songs without Words!* They're about the only thing I can play on the piano." "I like *On Wings of Song*, because I hear it so much on the radio." "Anyway, I know it's the *Mendelssohn Wedding March* you march *out* by."

Wolfgang Amadeus Mozart (pronounced Moh-tsahrt). Austrian. B. Salzburg, 1756; d. Vienna, 1791. "The Wonder Child." Possibly the greatest natural genius in the history of music, and the youngest of prodigies to compose and play in public. He set new standards in the fields of opera, the symphony, and chamber music. An inspired melodist, he also developed a technique and a perfection of style seldom equaled. His early death was a tragedy, all the more since his genius was far from appreciated during his lifetime. "If I had a child, I certainly wouldn't bring him up that way. No wonder he turned out sickly." "Maybe if his father had taught him a few practical things instead of just music, he would have done better." "But what a charming personality it must have been! Kissing the queen and all that!" "I believe he was poisoned by a jealous rival." "I'm sure that *Don Juan* music is lovely, even though you never hear it." "He wrote his three great symphonies inside of six weeks, and in summer too!" "I always say if you can play Mozart, you can play anything." "It looks like the easiest music, but it's really the most difficult. That's because it takes *style*."

[164]

Franz Schubert. Austrian. B. Vienna, 1797; d. Vienna, 1828. "Creator of the *Lied*." Another natural genius cut off by an untimely death. Most famous as a song-writer, the first to show the possibilities of "art-song." Schubert wrote over 600 songs, but also ten symphonies and much other music. He was without a doubt the fastest worker in musical history, yet so bad a business man that he died practically penniless. His *Erlking* was composed at the age of eighteen, and he was only twenty-five when he wrote the *Unfinished Symphony*. "This is not the Schubert that wrote *The Bee*, that Jack Benny tries to play. That one's name was François." "I'm so glad Romberg wrote *Blossom Time*, because now I know all about Franz Schubert." "The *Song of Love* is taken from the *Unfinished Symphony*, you know." "I never can tell his *Ave Maria* from the one by Gounod till the violinist begins to play octaves."

Robert Schumann. German. B. Zwickau, 1810; d. Bonn, 1856. "The Philosopher." Perhaps the most important composer of the early romantic school, who not only expressed its fundamental ideas in his music but succeeded also in interpreting them through his writings. He emphasized human and emotional values at all times and commanded a musical idiom that was highly original and full of melodic inspiration. Far more thoughtful than most of his contemporaries, he nevertheless lost his reason and died at a comparatively early age. His love for Clara Wieck, who eventually became his wife, was the great passion of his life. Schumann was a

[165]

great song-writer, but his four symphonies also rank high, and his piano music is as fine as any that has been written. "I never can tell the difference between Schubert and Schumann. Maybe I ought to listen to their music more carefully." "What I like about Schumann is that he was nice to Brahms and Chopin, and they are practically my favorite composers." "Wasn't Schumann one of the few music critics who could really play and compose?" "Anyway, he wrote *The Happy Farmer*, and that's one of the first pieces I learned." "I always say that if you can play Schumann, you can play anything." *died 1957*

Jean Sibelius. Finnish. B. Tavastehus, 1865. "The Lone Rock." Shares with two other S's, Richard Strauss and Stravinsky, the position of outstanding importance among living composers. At the age of seventy-four he is still active, having completed an eighth symphony recently. A radio poll selected him as the most popular of the serious composers on the air. This popularity rests largely on the tone poem, *Finlandia*, and the melancholy *Valse Triste*, but his great symphonies are constantly becoming better known. He lives and works in solitude in his native Finland. "That's the composer that Werner Janssen conducted so well, isn't it? Janssen was so nice looking. And now he's married Ann Harding." "His music sounds bleak and rugged, like his own Finland. It's very strong, but I don't quite understand it." "I didn't know they had any music in Finland—only fish and long-distance runners."

Richard Strauss. German. B. Munich, 1864. "Successor to Wagner and Liszt." Although now retired for some time, the aging Strauss still produces music occasionally. He has lived to see his symphonic poems established as classics, and he is rated among the world's greatest song-writers. His operas go beyond the innovations of Wagner, but while they are more sensational and astonishing, they do not show a comparable inspiration. However, *Der Rosenkavalier* can be called the world's greatest musical comedy next to *Die Meistersinger*. "I heard Strauss conduct when he was in this country. But I like Stokowski better." "They say he composed *Traum durch die Dämmerung* while he was waiting for his wife to put on her hat." "*Heldenleben* is supposed to be his own life. He is the hero, and I don't mean maybe." "I like where the trombones come in in *Don Juan*." "The question is whether it is legitimate to use a wind-machine for the windmills in *Don Quixote*." "After all, *Till Eulenspiegel* is the best of the symphonic poems. Give me a villain instead of a hero every time."

Igor Stravinsky. Russian. B. Oranienbaum, 1882. "Master of the Ballet." The most brilliant of the modernists, with the advantage of having his music used largely as accompaniment to stage ballets, which naturally increase its effectiveness. There are authentic touches of genius in this music, and it is practically attuned to modern ears. *The Firebird* has become very popular, and *Petrouschka* seems almost obvious to-day. The rest of Stravinsky is still debatable material, much of it undeniably important. "I wish he didn't try to write ragtime. The man has no conception of jazz whatever." "But did you ever hear such gorgeous orchestration?" "That barbaric rhythm in *Rites of Spring* makes one wonder how far civilization has advanced after all." "I liked Bolm and Massine in *Petrouschka*. They made it so vivid." "Have you seen Vera Zorina in 'I Married an Angel'?"

Peter Iljitch Tschaikowsky (pronounced Chai-koff'-skee). Russian. B. Votinsk, 1840; d. St. Petersburg (Leningrad), 1896. "The Melancholy Russian." Often belittled because of his obvious sentimentality and self-pity, Tschaikowsky has established his permanent significance in music with three symphonies, two concertos, and several smaller works, among which the *Romeo and Juliet Fantasy Overture* is outstandingly and deservedly popular. His *Symphonie Pathétique* is one of the best known in the world, with the individual distinction of ending in a melancholy mood, following a triumphant march movement. Tschaikowsky was supported through his best creative years by a woman whom he never met in person, Nadejda von Meck. Their correspondence is preserved in the book, *Beloved Friend*, by Catherine Drinker Bowen. "I always think sad music is the best, don't you?" "There must have been *something* somebody could have done for him." "Well, if he can make me cry, let him go ahead. I'm willing."

Giuseppe Verdi. Italian. B. Le Roncole, 1813; d. Busseto, 1901. "The Grand Old Man." By far the best and most prolific of the opera composers, excluding

Wagner, who is in a class by himself. Verdi's *Aïda* is "the perfect opera" and will never lose its appeal. *Otello* and *Falstaff*, written in his old age, are distinctly more elaborate than the earlier works in their musical technique. *Il Trovatore*, *La Traviata*, and *Rigoletto* all contain tunes that the public loves, and may be considered light music on the whole. "I like Verdi because you can just sit back and wait for the arias." "If you saw melodramatic plots like that on the stage, you'd walk right out on them. It's only the music that puts them over." "*Aïda* was written for the opening of the Suez Canal. Can you imagine an opera for the opening of the *Erie Canal?*"

Richard Wagner. German. B. Leipzig, 1813; d. Venice, 1883. "Creator of Music Drama." Born in the same year as Verdi, he revolutionized grand opera while the Italian was merely producing better examples of the old type. Wagner was a rebel politically as well as musically, long exiled from Germany for his views. He eventually got the backing from the "mad king" of Bavaria to carry out his ideas of "music drama," something far greater than opera, with a continuous flow of orchestral music, no set arias, and with supermen, gods, and demigods as characters. He carried out his intentions in every detail, meanwhile behaving detestably in private life. There is nothing in music to compare with the series of music dramas created by Richard Wagner. "Borrowing money was bad enough, but when it came to his friends' wives!" "I never can believe Wagner wrote anything as familiar as the *Wedding March*." "He was paid $5,000 to compose a march for the Philadelphia Centennial, and it was pretty poor." "Well, if he were alive today, you'd probably fall for him the same as everybody else." "It takes mature, solid singers to do that difficult music. You can't expect everything."

That ought to give you enough material for an ordinary musical conversation. If you are not sure of your ground, try to pin the other person down and see how accurate his or her information really is. "As, for instance?" is always a legitimate question. It is so easy to babble with vague enthusiasm and throw in a word like "nuance" from time to time.

YOU CAN BE ACCURATE

Actually, the general outlines of musical history are not hard to keep straight. There are interesting parallels to the development of the other arts, particularly painting and literature.

Always you have the slow process of pioneering, up to the point where a recognized medium of expression is established. Every human being goes through some such process, discovering ways of becoming articulate, ways of producing effects that may be of interest to others, ways finally of transferring thoughts, moods, and emotions through the medium of tone or color or language.

Everybody is perfectly capable of having such thoughts, moods, and emotions. But it is only the artist who succeeds in expressing them so that other human beings are inevitably (though not always immediately) aware of his meaning. This always implies the mastery of some technique of expression, and in many cases this is the only difference between the artist and the average person. We can all enjoy something of the same feelings, even if we are unable to express them, and similarly we can enjoy the expression of them by someone who has mastered the technique of communication, although completely ignorant of how this miracle is achieved.

The history of every art shows that, once a technique was perfected, it became of paramount importance to both the creators and the interpreters of that art. In this way you arrive at the "classical school" of any form of artistic expression, the method that emphasized form and style and perfection of detail, often at the expense of honest emotion and human sincerity.

CLASSICS CAN BE HUMAN

The classic perfectionists of music are mostly forgotten because they had little or nothing to say. Such supreme technicians as Bach, Haydn, and Mozart are remembered because there was so much more to their music than a merely formal and technical beauty.

Beethoven stands at the end of the eighteenth and the beginning of the nineteenth century and marks also the dividing line between the classic and romantic schools of music. His technical ability was enormous, but he considered the direct expression of emotion and the human drama (or comedy) of far greater importance. He put new life into the classic form of the symphony, and he could make even a string quartet express tremendous conflicts of human feeling. Strangely enough, his one opera, *Fidelio*, turned out to be formal and artificial as compared with the naturalism that was later developed, and when he heretically put human voices into his final symphony, he treated them cruelly, as though they were the inanimate instruments whose possibilities he knew so much better. But without Beethoven the music of the nineteenth and twentieth centuries would have been impossible.

BEGINNINGS OF ROMANTICISM

Franz Schubert, who died only a year later than Beethoven, showed little of the gigantic intellect or the revolutionary methods of the older genius. Yet he was a romantic composer in the best sense, depending upon instinct and a natural musicianship for self-expression, rather than upon the technique of the classic masters. His great contribution to music was as a song-writer, and in this field he still stands supreme, not only as a pioneer, but as a genius who could express an amazing variety of ideas with an equally amazing economy of materials. Schubert achieved no startling orchestral effects, although at least two of his symphonies have attained immortality. His unique contribution was in establishing the possibilities of the song form and in his rare gift of expressing a complete thought or a satisfying emotion within the compass of a short and comparatively simple piece of music, vocal or instrumental.

In the actual substitution of the romantic ideal for the classic, Robert Schumann was of far greater importance. He also made a specialty of song-writing and the smaller instrumental forms (particularly piano music), but his melodies were more original, his harmonies were richer and more varied, his underlying ideas were profounder and full of a deep, human philosophy. He was able not only to express this romanticism in his music, but to write about it articulately and to discover and encourage its potentialities in others. The names of Chopin and Brahms might never have acquired their full significance without the early recognition and continued influence of Schumann.

THE ROMANTIC SCHOOL DEVELOPS

Mendelssohn, contemporary with Schumann but of even shorter life, belongs definitely in the romantic group, although, like Schubert, he depended largely upon extraordinary natural gifts and occupied himself little with revolutionary ideas or methods. He was the first of the romanticists to discover the real significance of Bach, and his efforts actually rescued that supreme genius from complete oblivion. Mendelssohn wrote well in all the forms of music except opera. His brilliant *Overture* to *A Midsummer Night's Dream* remains a monument to his youthful precocity, while his oratorio, *The Elijah*, assures the immortality of his maturer creative work.

[173]

Poland's greatest composer, Chopin, is the ideal of all pianists and lovers of piano music, practically concentrating his efforts on that one instrument. But his wonderful originality and the highly personal character of all his musical expression would place him high among the world's composers in general, regardless of his unique mastery of the keyboard. Chopin first discovered the possibilities of decoration and embellishment in the creation of tone color, and the characteristic ornamentation of his individual melodies led directly to the later impressionism of Debussy and his followers.

THE GIANTS OF OPERA

The two great masters of operatic music—Verdi and Wagner—were born in the same year (1813), but the Italian outlived the German by nearly two decades. Wagner's development of the elaborate form of opera known as "music drama" places him above and apart from all conventional dramatic composers. He practically eliminated the old-fashioned style of set arias, duets, and choruses, making his music a continuous flow, with emphasis on the orchestra rather than the voices, and using musical labels, or "Leitmotifs"—*i.e.* short melodic slogans—to identify his characters and other important features. Verdi adhered more strictly to the routine style, although eventually influenced by Wagner, and unquestionably carried Italian opera to its highest level musically and dramatically.

[174]

Franz Liszt, who was the father-in-law of Wagner, contributed much to the career of the younger composer, not only producing his early works in defiance of public disapproval, but actually creating many of the "motifs" that Wagner utilized. His brilliancy as a concert pianist outshone his creative abilities, but his invention of the Symphonic Poem gives him a high place in the romantic school of composition.

Johannes Brahms, who was brought into artificial rivalry with Wagner by their short-sighted contemporaries, is today recognized as the most important composer of absolute music since Beethoven and Bach, an ideal combination of the classic and the romantic. His four symphonies may be considered the climax of that form, and his concertos for the piano and the violin are of equal significance. Brahms is outstanding also as a song-writer and composer of chamber music (string quartets, trios, etc.).

SENTIMENTAL AND SPECTACULAR

The symphonies of the Russian Tschaikowsky are perhaps more popular than even those of Brahms, chiefly because of the spectacular character of his orchestration and the sentimental appeal of his melodies. In this tendency toward sentimentality Tschaikowsky represents the extreme of the romantic style of composition, far removed from the strict formulas of classicism.

César Franck, Belgian by birth and French by residence, has also contributed one exceedingly popular

[175]

symphony to romantic music, with more than a touch of modernism in his harmonies and the freedom of his technique. But the real founder of the modern school is the French composer, Debussy, whose songs, piano music, and orchestral works, along with the unique opera, *Pelléas and Mélisande*, established the principles of harmony and tone color that are universally accepted today. His music is analogous to the "impressionism" of painting and literature, definitely beyond even the most revolutionary ideas of the romantic school.

Also of the rather advanced modern type is Richard Strauss, who elaborated the technique of Wagner in his operas and improved considerably on the symphonic poems of Liszt. He stands high also among the great song-writers of the world.

MODERN AND ULTRAMODERN

The Russian Stravinsky is the most important of the ultramodernists, from the creative standpoint, with the spectacular field of the ballet his particular stamping-ground. Finland's modern genius, Sibelius, is more conservative, yet sufficiently advanced in his ideas of harmony, form, and instrumentation. He represents the latest and most complex version of the classic symphony and other absolute music.

If you become interested in the composers of great music, you will probably enjoy finding out more and more about their lives and how they came to write their immortal compositions. But the music itself is always more important than the man who wrote it, and if your enthusiasm does not begin with listening and perhaps taking part in the actual works, you might as well concentrate on the lives of any famous personages of history. The real fun in the biographical approach may be found in the possibility of saying, at a first hearing, "That sounds like Bach" or "That is surely Beethoven" or "That could not have been written by anyone but Debussy." General styles and individual characteristics become steadily clearer and more recognizable as your listening habits develop, and once you feel really at home among the great composers, you have added quite definitely to the satisfactions of life.

APPRAISAL OF PERFORMANCE

You can listen to a symphony or a sonata intelligently if you know or come to recognize the principal tunes. There are always at least two tunes in the first movement or section, and they stand out clearly near the start. In the middle there is a great deal of confusion which only the experienced listener will unravel, and at the end you will hear the tunes again, quite clearly.

This is the general outline of "sonata form," which appears regularly at the start of a sonata, symphony, string quartet, quintet, or trio, and often elsewhere in absolute or pure music. Its two outstanding tunes are like the hero and heroine of a play or a novel. They show a similar contrast, one having a masculine and the other a feminine character, and they appear in two different but related keys.

The development of this melodic material, sometimes called the "free fantasia," corresponds to the plot of the play or novel. The tunes are carried through all sorts of adventures. They are broken up, turned upside down, transferred to various instruments and keys, until one wonders what will happen next. Their eventual return, or "recapitulation," whole and unharmed, constitutes a happy or at least a logical ending, with perhaps a "coda" or tailpiece to give the final blessing. "Sonata form" is not hard to follow if you remember the tunes.

The second movement of a symphony or sonata is generally slow and is likely to have one outstanding melody, which again is easily followed. There may be "variations" on this melody, which are merely decorations and embellishments, the serious equivalent to the improvisations of swing.

A sonata has only three movements, with a lively *Finale*, but a symphony has four, inserting a *Scherzo*, or jocular movement, which originally had the form of a *Minuet*. In such movements the tunes also stand out prominently.

WHY NOT APPLAUD?

It has become a tradition of the concert hall (and of the NBC broadcasts) not to applaud between the movements of a symphony, perhaps on the theory that there is some connecting thread that should not be broken.

Actually, this is seldom true. There may be some definite relationship of keys, but the moods are contrasted and the arrangement generally follows a conventional formula. Seldom does a composer indicate that one movement is to lead directly into the next, and seldom does a conductor continue without that embarrassed and embarrassing pause, broken only by scattered coughs, a perceptible fidgeting in the chairs of players as well as listeners, and perhaps a furtive bit of tuning somewhere on the stage. There are a few symphonies that bring back earlier themes or tunes in the final movement—notably that of César Franck, the *Ninth* of Beethoven, and Dvorak's *From the New World*. But even this "cyclic" form does not prevent a pause or applause between movements.

Critics generally comment on the tempo of a conductor, agreeing or disagreeing with him as to the speed at which each movement should be played. Beyond this, they are interested chiefly in whether the notes are correctly performed and whether the instrumental balance brings out the details properly.

OPERA HAS ITS ADVANTAGES

An opera is easier for the novice than a symphony, for the music has all the advantages of words, action, and scenery. Except in Wagner, the leading melodies stand out very clearly, and even his earlier operas are full of set tunes. It is well to acquaint oneself with the story of an opera before hearing it. Absurd as it may be, it still clarifies what goes on on the stage. Confidentially, a good light opera or musical comedy is greatly to be preferred to a dull grand opera.

Standards of interpretation are difficult to determine in music. Personality and the tricks of showmanship count for so much that even an experienced listener is easily deceived. It is fair to say that the interpreter should transfer to the audience exactly what the composer meant to express. But if most of the listeners do not know what that was, they are at a distinct disadvantage.

Toscanini has built up his unique reputation as a conductor by sticking absolutely to the letter of the score and taking no liberties whatever. He interprets a symphony with such perfection of detail that nothing else is needed. Practically all other conductors make some use of prima-donna methods, either in their actions with the baton or in the musical effects they produce. When the eye sees the conductor going through motions that dramatize the music, such as lifting both hands to high heaven, trembling, that naturally helps the listener to get the spirit of the performance.

ARTISTS OR ACROBATS?

Pianists and violinists also make gestures that are unnecessary but seem to be demanded by a drama-loving public. If, however, you watch Kreisler or Heifetz on the stage, you will realize that a violinist does not have to sway or bend over or otherwise draw attention to himself. It is enough to play the music beautifully.

Singers have the greatest temptation to turn on the personality and forget about artistic integrity. It is an open question how far facial expression and even gesture may be permitted on the concert stage, but certainly no one likes a singer of the "dead-pan" type. Obvious exaggerations should be avoided, and they are the besetting sin of the more popular type of singing.

Scooping from one note to another; whining; a hard, nasal tone; sudden changes of quality, particularly, opening wide on a low and presumably emotional note, coming in just off the beat, hanging on to a tone longer than is necessary, breaking it up with the insertion of extra syllables—these are only a few of the offenses against good taste committed by popular singers. The one thing they can teach concert artists, however, is clear enunciation. You do understand the words from one of those ballad-swinging jazz babies.

STANDARDS OF GOOD SINGING

Correctness of pitch; a clear, steady tone of good quality, without a wobble; and the ability to project words and a mood—this much should be demanded of any singer. How many of them actually live up to such a standard? It has been suggested that if the singer seems to be comfortable, the audience feels the same way, and that is all anyone can ask. But a smile and a pretty face will go a long way in covering up vocal deficiencies, and many an instrumentalist has traded considerably on a foreign name and an accent.

[181]

The people who are the most critical of musical performances do not get the most fun out of them. Professional critics have their moments of enthusiasm, but in general they lead sad and disappointed lives. They would like to speak well of everything they hear, but they know that the really great performance is all too rare.

If you want to enjoy music as a listener, it is just as well not to be too critical. By the time you have developed real standards of taste, all the fun may have gone out of listening. You are fortunate in being able to turn a great deal of music on or off as you please, via radio, and you have a right to be honest about this and listen only to those things that give you sincere pleasure. If you are not trying to impose your taste on others, why should they impose theirs on you?

THE CREATIVE URGE

Dᴇᴇᴘ in the heart of every man there is the desire to create something. Even though there is plenty of creative work to be done in connection with even the most prosaic business, people generally want to be "artists" in a more conventional sense. Those who were once busily writing the Great American Play or Novel are now trying to turn out the Great American Song Hit.

Actually, it is possible for almost anyone to do some creative work in music. Children prove this at an early age, when they make up both the words and the tunes of little songs that fit into the games they are playing. It is rather primitive music, but it has its creative significance. Somebody will start chanting "Johnnie's got a new suit," or whatever it may be, and they all take it up and sing it rhythmically, in the true manner of folk-music.

Children are now being taught to compose tunes in kindergarten and the early school grades, and they find it easy. They can make up their tunes by ear long before they know anything about notes. Sets of bells are a help, for they are numbered and arrange themselves easily into patterns.

Once the significance of a musical pattern is clearly grasped, it is not difficult either to play or to compose a tune. Arthur Garbett, director of the Standard School Broadcasts, has been successful in using the pattern of the old five-tone scale, simply applying it to sets of words and rhythms already in existence. For instance, *America*, according to this pattern, could have a new setting as follows:

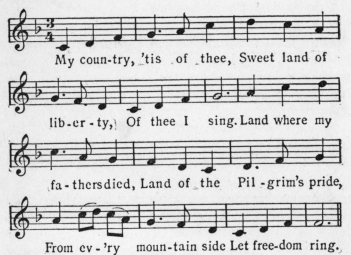

My coun-try, 'tis of thee, Sweet land of

lib-er-ty, Of thee I sing. Land where my

fa-thers died, Land of the Pil-grim's pride,

From ev-'ry moun-tain side Let free-dom ring.

(The five-tone scale here appears as both C, D, F, G, A and F, G, A, C, D, giving a range of one tone more than an octave. It could be carried on indefinitely if the voice were equal to it.)

With such a guide to melody, the individual soon finds it possible to be more and more original. Patterns of the diatonic scale and the major chord are common in all music, and they provide endless suggestions for complete melodies. It is possible to write a complete tune on as few as three notes. For instance, the first three notes of the scale might work out as follows in the key of G:

The easiest thing in the world is to take any poem (or piece of prose, for that matter) and set notes to it, simply following the natural rhythm of the words and giving the longer and perhaps the higher notes to the more important words. You can make a game of this by

[185]

simply juggling the numbers from one to eight (or possibly nine or ten) and then picking them blindly for the successive words. Or let each member of the group call out a number between one and ten and write these numbers in over the words of the poem. The result will be very similar to some of the modern substitutes for serious song-writing, and generally pretty terrible.

Just being able to put notes to a text is by no means composition; but if it amuses you, there is no harm in it. The commonest trick is to take a rhymed and metrical verse and set it musically so that the accents fall as though it were prose. ("Hew to the line, let the accents fall where they will.") For instance, *America* could be prosaically rewritten like this:

My coun-try, 'tis of thee, Sweet land of lib-er-ty, Of thee I sing. Land where my fa-thers died, Land of the Pil-grim's pride, From ev-'ry mountain side Let free-dom ring.

(Most people will prefer the metrical and melodious setting to which they are accustomed.)

If children are encouraged in their first efforts at creative music, as well as in trying to play and sing, there is no telling how far they may go in time. That was the way Mozart and all the other prodigies began, and even the nonprodigies can produce something in the way of self-expression. It may not be worth listening to, but it comes under the head of musical composition just the same.

CHILDREN ARE GOOD COMPOSERS

Writing little songs, both words and music, is not hard for the average child, as has been proved many times. All that is needed, as a rule, is a subject, and an active imagination does the rest. It may be necessary for the child to dictate the tune, but successful popular composers have been known to do that, too.

After experiments with vocal music, the composition of little marches and waltzes should not be difficult either, especially if these rhythms have become familiar through the ear and possibly through performance. After that it should soon be clear whether a child actually has any creative ability or not.

The one thing that everyone would naturally like to write is a popular song hit. Even serious composers have confessed as much in moments of complete honesty. (Charles Wakefield Cadman may resent the reputation he acquired through *The Land of the Sky Blue Water* and *At*

Dawning, but he could not possibly resent the financial returns.)

It is a great mistake to think that popular songs are easy to write. They have a definite technique, and it takes experience and a rather special gift to turn them out with any consistent success.

SO YOU WANT TO WRITE A SONG

There is no harm in trying to write a popular song. It is an interesting hobby. But anyone thinking seriously of achieving bona fide publication should realize that the chances are enormously against him.

Most popular publishers refuse even to look at an unsolicited manuscript. They have more than enough material as it is, and they see no reason to spend money on an unknown name, even if a song seems good. Moreover, they have a deadly terror of nuisance suits brought by misguided or deliberately dishonest people who fancy or pretend that they see similarities between their manuscript and a published hit. It is safer not to look at anything at all except the work of staff writers and composers well known to the publishers.*

In spite of this well-known condition, a type of racketeer known as the "song shark" feeds upon the

* There is one recognized clearinghouse, The Songmart, 220 West 42nd St., New York City, which legitimately brings the amateur song-writer to the attention of the publisher, although most of its work consists in kindly criticism and a tactful discouragement that saves its clients both disappointment and money in the long run.

[188]

gullible amateur and has taken large quantities of his money under absolutely false pretenses. Beware of people who agree to set music to your words or vice versa and then secure publication of your song. They merely intend to bleed you for what they can, knowing perfectly well that at best a song-writer's living is precarious. Some of these "sharks" are gradually finding their way into jail, where they belong.

But suppose you want to write a popular song just for the fun of it. Why not at least write it correctly (even if you have to call in a musician to help you) so that if a publisher ever should see it, he would not be horrified at your obvious ignorance of the fundamentals?

Did you know, for instance, that a publisher or a band leader practically insists that your chorus shall have exactly thirty-two measures of music? This is not merely a conveniently balanced form. It is a definite aid to timing on the radio.

TWO'S COMPANY IN MUSIC

All measured music works out in multiples of two, and the popular chorus is the most conventional of musical forms. Its real unit is a sequence of eight measures, generally called a "theme." This may consist of two identical phrases of four measures each, or it may be a continuous and complete melody. Whatever it is, the "theme" is likely to be repeated immediately, thus completing the first half of the chorus and coming to what amounts to a full stop.

Then comes a middle section of eight measures of contrasting quality, generally in a different key from the main theme. This is called the "release" or *B* section (the "theme" being known as *A*). Finally, the theme is brought back for one more repetition, completing the thirty-two measures. This works out as a very definite form, *A-A-B-A*, and you will be surprised at the number of popular choruses that follow it literally. Jerome Kern's *Smoke Gets in Your Eyes* is an excellent example, and so is Gershwin's *The Man I Love*.

SONGS HAVE A THEME CENTER

Obviously, the *A* section, or theme, is a very important part of any popular chorus, for it generally appears three times, making up twenty-four of the total thirty-two measures of music. Sometimes the arrangement is *A-B-A-B*, or even *A-B-A-C*, but the theme is practically sure to be repeated at least once.

Infringement suits, claiming plagiarism (mostly based upon absolutely accidental similarities), almost always concentrate on these eight important measures. There is a mistaken idea that one is allowed to borrow up to four measures of music, perhaps because it takes that much to make the body of a theme. But the law forbids the taking of anything "essential" or "substantial," and it is generally up to the judge to decide just what those words mean.

The question is often asked, "Which is written first, the music or the words?" In the most successful popular songs, the two are likely to be composed together, in collaboration. Stephen Foster developed his songs a phrase at a time, thinking of the words and music simultaneously. Such teams as the Gershwins, Rodgers and Hart, Schwartz and Dietz, and Gordon and Revel have followed much the same technique in their most successful songs. Two heads are better than one in popular song-writing.

THINKING IN PLATITUDES

It is strange how consistently the amateur song-writer uses the same old verbal expressions and the same old melodic progressions that have been heard so many times that the public is sick of them. He naïvely writes down such cosmic thoughts as "I love you," "You are the one for me," "With you in the moonlight," "You are so sweet," etc., etc., *ad infinitum* and *ad nauseam*. Often he puts his thoughts into waltz time, which is the hardest to sell, because people dance very few waltzes nowadays.

The novice should remember that, to attract any attention whatsoever, he must write something actually better or more striking than the work of the average professional. He is not likely to accomplish this by merely repeating the platitudes that are already a drug on the market.

SAY IT IN A DIFFERENT WAY

The secret of most popular songs today is an unusual twist of words, plus an unusual twist of melody. There is really only one universal topic of interest, which is summed up in the words "I love you" But this fundamental idea can be expressed in a great variety of ways. Irving Berlin gave it a new twist when he used the familiar phrase, *I'm putting all my eggs in one basket*. He suggested it by the picturesque title, *Cheek to Cheek*. When he wrote *I've got my love to keep me warm*, he not only gave a new twist to an old thought, but his melody introduced almost immediately a strain of real originality.

So the first big victory is won when you arrive at a striking and rather original phrase, with the notes fitting so perfectly that the association of words and music is practically inevitable. Here again Irving Berlin showed his skill in creating short titles that had the effect of slogans, like *What'll I Do?*, *All Alone*, *Always*, and *Remember;* and people did remember the songs by those short phrases.

EMPHASIZING THE TITLE

A publisher likes to have the title phrase appear not only at the start of a chorus but again at the finish. He prints this phrase in capitals as a reminder. To make this repetition logical is quite a trick, but it can be done, and it helps to make the chorus seem practical.

Once the opening phrase is established (covering perhaps four measures) it should not be hard to stretch it out into a complete theme of eight measures, coming only to a half-stop or "incomplete cadence." The repetition then merely demands a new line of words with the necessary rhymes.

In the middle section, the words as well as the music should offer some contrast. There is almost necessarily a change of key, and the mood changes with it. Jerome Kern again accomplished this very cleverly in *Smoke gets in your eyes*, and so did George Gershwin in *The Man I Love*, which helps to make these two of the best popular songs ever written.

The problem then is merely to modulate back to the original key for the final repetition of the opening theme, closing if possible with the words of the title (as in both the songs just mentioned). There should be some special punch in this closing line, giving a point to the entire chorus.

THE VERSE IS SECONDARY

If you have a good chorus of thirty-two (sometimes sixty-four) measures you don't have to worry much about the verse. It should never be more than half as long as the chorus. Some modern songs limit the verse to eight measures, and some drop it out altogether (as Cole Porter did in *Night and Day*, which simply had an extra-long chorus). By the time a song gets arranged for dancing, radio, and recording, it is hard to distinguish one part from another anyway. The only real significance of a verse is that it sets the stage for the chorus, builds up to it, and prepares the listener's mind for it. Musically it should be of rather different character, but not in a different rhythm. (Old-fashioned songs would often start in what we would call fox-trot time, and then

[193]

change to a waltz; but you can't do that today. The tempo and rhythm have to be constant for dancing purposes.)*

It is now literally impossible to write a completely original tune of potential popularity. With only seven different notes in the diatonic scale, and twelve in the chromatic, accidental similarities are bound to occur, and basic patterns of melody continue to turn up with surprising frequency. To be absolutely safe from any accusations of plagiarism, it is actually advisable to have in mind some definite model "in the public domain," and such a basis will as a rule produce a better tune than bona fide "inspiration." If you go back deliberately to the classics or folk-music, you not only protect yourself against the nuisances and the racketeers of the music business, but you are likely to produce a pretty good piece of music, since its fundamental value has already been proved.

WHY BE COMPLETELY ORIGINAL?

Actually, originality can be the least of your worries in writing a popular song. If it is based on some old pattern or an established classic of the dim past, consciously or unconsciously, so much the better. A publisher is not likely to let it get into print if there is any danger of infringement on a copyrighted number.

* An excellent little book of practical advice along these lines, particularly in regard to the approach to the publishers, is *So You Want to Write a Song*, by Robert Bruce (Mayfair Publications).

Getting a publisher sufficiently interested to print your song is a far greater problem. The best procedure is to have it sung on every possible occasion, trying it out on disinterested listeners, perhaps broadcasting it over a local radio station. This is not really difficult, and it is the best way to find out if the song has any value. When the music stores begin to get some bona fide requests for it, you can be fairly sure that a publisher will soon take notice.

THE MEANING OF ASCAP

If you are ever fortunate enough to have five numbers published, you become eligible for membership in the American Society of Composers, Authors and Publishers, an organization that collects license fees from all the users of commercially profitable music and distributes the income in the form of royalties to its members, according to classification. Unquestionably ASCAP, as it is familiarly known, is a blessing not only to the American creator of popular music (who would otherwise be deprived of the performing rights to which he is entitled under the Federal Copyright Law) but also to the various interests for whom music is a staple and profitable commodity. These entertainment enterprises, including radio, the theater, restaurants, night clubs and dance halls, absolutely need a clearing-house that assures them of the right to use copyrighted music without fear of litigation on the part of either its creators or its publishers.

Most of those who try their hand at writing popular songs cannot expect to arrive at publication or the glory of ASCAP membership. But they can at least have the fun of expressing themselves in a way that has a wide appeal, and they might as well try to do it in a fashion that conforms to the traditions and the regulations of the skilled professionals. Song-writing can be a fascinating pastime, but it is a mistake to think of it in professional terms unless one has both the special gift and the special experience, plus perhaps an inside track to the back door of a publisher who is willing to spend the money and time and effort to "plug" a song into what is at best a rather artificial success.

GENIUS, TALENT, AND ORDINARY INTELLIGENCE

JUST because this book has encouraged you to get fun out of music by playing it, listening to it, and even composing it in a small way, don't get yourself confused with the real artists of either the interpretive or the creative type. There is a vast difference between the person who can derive some personal enjoyment from self-expression through music and the one who definitely gives pleasure to others by a combination of special talent and hard work. Beyond this it is still a long way to that inspired individual whom the world recognizes sooner or later as a genius.

The analogy of language and literature should again be helpful in making these distinctions. Anyone at all can learn to speak, read, and write his own language. In precisely the same way, anyone at all can learn to sing or play, to read and to write music. There is no mystery about it. There are sounds, to be produced by the normal voice, or upon instruments that one learns to play as one learns to use a typewriter. There are letters of the alphabet representing those sounds, but only seven of them, from A to G, as compared with the twenty-six in the English alphabet. There are lines upon which notes are written, just as easily learned as ordinary penmanship. So there is nothing in reading or writing the language of music that is beyond the grasp of the ordinary intelligence.

But so strong is the tradition of mystery in music that people actually look with amazement upon the simple ability to write out a succession of notes that make sense. Even those who have learned how to do it frequently deceive themselves into thinking that this logical progression actually has some creative significance.

A THOUGHT FOR COMPOSERS

Of all the English that is being written every day, in the form of letters, reports, themes, or exercises, how much is worth taking seriously as literature? How much that actually gets into print is really worth printing, from the literary standpoint?

Anybody at all can write a book, for it simply means putting together a certain number of words in adequately correct sentences. But how many such books would be worth reading?

Anybody at all can learn in time to write a symphony that will be technically correct, but how many people will want to listen to it? Even in the field of interpretation, it is fair to say that most of those who speak their own language perfectly well are not likely to be in demand as public readers or orators or dramatic actors. There is the same difference between the average interpreter of the language of music and the highly trained performer acceptable to an audience.

The reading of music can and should become a national habit, just like the reading of books. It is a perfectly simple matter to take at least a piano or vocal score, and possibly even an orchestral piece, and read it as one would read a page of print, without ever going near a piano. The notes on a page, just like the words, represent definite sounds, and these sounds can be mentally heard, as you subconsciously hear the words when you read a story to yourself. You can develop the ability to hear complete harmonies and even instrumental quality by simply reading the notes to yourself.

A THOUGHT FOR PERFORMERS

Beware of the danger of thinking that, just because you can sing or play a little, other people necessarily want to listen to you. They will generally let you know if they do, and if you are really worth hearing, your reputation will grow fast enough. But beware even more of the temptation to look at any notes you may have written down as being actually worth playing. Don't trust your friends either, for they are almost sure to be complimentary and overwhelmed with astonishment that you could actually write music. If your work has any real merit, it will eventually come to the notice of an unprejudiced

[199]

observer, and the final answer will always be at the box office or its equivalent.

There are professional creators and interpreters of music struggling along today, seemingly unaware that their work has only a limited commercial value. They have both talent and industry, but they lack that indefinable spark that would place them among the elect. Often it is a question of "personality" or "temperament" or whatever you wish to call it. Splendid, well-trained artists have failed to capture an audience because of their lack of showmanship and nothing else.

In the presence of genius, however, one realizes that showmanship in the ordinary sense is unnecessary. Personality and temperament are there by nature, not artificially created. True greatness in an artist is indefinable, but it is also unmistakable; and the greatest artists are generally the simplest and most unpretentious of human beings.

NATURE'S MUSICAL HANDYMEN

One hears a great deal about "natural" musicians, people who play and often improvise "by ear" and sometimes boast that they "can't read a note of music." They can all do amusing things by instinct, and might have done something significant if they had worked and studied. But perhaps they are better off as they are. At least they get more fun out of music that way.

Stephen Foster was a natural musician, with the peculiar gift of combining simple words and melodies in a way that sounded inevitable. (This apparent inevitability seems to be a distinguishing mark of all great music, no matter how much a composer may have experimented before arriving at the effect he wanted.) It would probably have been a mistake to turn Foster into a symphonic or operatic composer. He was supreme in the things he did, and a more elaborate musical education might well have ruined the directness of his inspirations.

On the other hand, it should be remembered that every great composer and interpreter of music was fundamentally a "natural" musician, generally starting as an infant prodigy. In spite of enormous gifts, which revealed themselves at a very early age, these outstanding geniuses all went through the hardest and most rigorous training. Those who became concert performers practiced for hours at a time upon their chosen instruments and were generally technical marvels at the age of ten or twelve. Those who had the creative urge first learned to play several instruments well, studied all the important music that had been written before their time, and waded through dreary text-books to command all the resources of harmony and counterpoint.

DISMISSING A DELUSION

Nobody ever wrote great music as the result of pure inspiration. It was always the result of painstaking study, careful workmanship, and the minutest attention to detail, plus an inherent gift that the composer himself could not have explained.

[201]

Bach and Haydn were completely naïve about their musical inspirations. They credited God and let it go at that. Beethoven was fiercely personal in his attitude, resenting the handicaps that nature and society visited upon him, insisting upon his own aristocracy of the brain.

Mozart took a frank delight in his own artistry and was perhaps too much aware of his extraordinary genius to please his jealous contemporaries. Schubert simply poured out music as though he could not help himself. He would make a song out of almost any poem, starting another just as soon as he had finished one, and never bothering about financial returns. He was so "natural" a composer that he rather neglected the details of workmanship in his constant frenzy of creation.

PHILOSOPHY AND EGOTISM

Schumann was far more introspective, philosophical, often filled with doubts as to his ability and inclined to analyze his own work. He composed best when he was happy in the love of his wife. Wagner was the sublime egotist among composers, but his egotism was justified, and he carried out every one of his intentions to the letter. He is the best example of the conscious artist who deliberately plans his effects and then realizes them ruthlessly, regardless of what or whom he might sacrifice in the process.

Brahms, on the other hand, was modest and seemingly doubtful of his ability, although in his heart he must have known when he had produced a great composition. His scholarship and tremendous industry have always been recognized, but unquestionably he had his full share of pure inspiration also.

The proper appreciation of true genius need not be affected by the habit of getting fun out of music. Brahms himself had his moments of relaxation, and the greatest artists of today have been known to unbend in their lighter moments and indulge in musical jokes, just as Papa Haydn did, all the way back in the eighteenth century.

NO DISRESPECT INTENDED

An informal attitude toward music need not interfere with the respect or even the reverence that is accorded a great performance or a great composition. Music can be taken seriously enough by those who honestly enjoy it. But they do not have to take it *hard*. The mere fact that you have made some attempt to play or sing, possibly even to compose a piece of music, should make you all the more aware of what has been achieved by both the interpreter and the creator of great music, inspiringly performed. You will get a special thrill if you are familiar with the composition and have perhaps tried to play it yourself. To that extent, the mere novice can commune with even the greatest geniuses of music.

JAZZ AND SWING SIMPLIFIED

T HERE was a vague impression that this book could be finished without going very deeply into the subject of popular music. People obviously get so much fun out of that branch of the art that no urging or analysis would seem necessary.

But a number of inquiries have made it evident that even serious music-lovers are anxious for some authentic information on the swing craze and its possibilities of permanence. Millions are frankly baffled by its manifestations, while still other millions surrender to its mysterious appeal without exactly knowing why. Comparatively few of the jitterbugs are thoroughly aware of the musical and psychological implications of their pet frenzy, even when they are quite familiar with the highly specialized lingo of the fraternity. It has already been suggested that jitterbugs develop a form of snobbery and exhibitionism not unlike that of the highbrow who talks technically and superciliously about symphonies, and it is fairly certain that the number of bona fide connoisseurs of swing is definitely limited.

There is, however, unquestionably a real technique to even the most extreme and apparently unruly examples of modern jazz, and the fundamentals of this technique can be grasped by the layman, regardless of his complete inability to participate in any way. It is not enough to dismiss the whole matter as a mere combination of exaggerated rhythmic emphasis and extraordinary skill in the playing of certain instruments, as was also suggested earlier in this book.

DEBUNKING THE SWING SNOBS

While much of the talk about the mysteries of swing is just as nonsensical and artificial as the similar bunkum solemnly retailed by the snobs of serious music, there are facts and technicalities decidedly worth explaining, and there is also some intrinsic factor that refuses to be explained or analyzed in any generally intelligible terms. George Simon, editor of the *Metronome*, whom I consider the outstanding authority on swing (and I am not overlooking those who have written scholarly or popular books on the subject), sums up the mystery in these words: "You can tell when you are being tickled, and what it is that tickles you. But can you explain or describe the *sensation of being tickled?*"

So it is not enough to say that swing consists of variations on popular tunes played with amazing skill and often improvised on the spot by musicians with a peculiar instinct for the rhythmic elaboration of a melodic line. There are musicians who can create and even improvise remarkable variations, perhaps of technical perfection, and who nevertheless are completely lacking in the subtle sense that makes real swing effective. The only way to explain this individual sense is to call it an apparent disregard of the natural beat of time based on a constant and inevitable awareness of its underlying influence. The great swing-players all do this by instinct, with varying degrees of beauty, depending upon their natural and acquired musical ability. The highly trained products of conventional music-teaching may not be able to do it at all.

Self-consciousness is a factor to be considered, and it is probably the lack of inhibitions, combined with a native feeling for rhythm, that makes Negro musicians in general better swing-players than white men are. When Benny Goodman gave his first concert in Carnegie Hall, the highly advertised "jam session," in which all the performers were supposed to indulge in extempore inspirations, turned out to be a flat failure, simply because they were all so self-conscious and so overawed by a new type of audience that they could not let themselves go.

Swing requires a complete abandonment to the mood of the moment. There must be an enormous technical facility in the background, but any suggestion of studied and deliberate scholarship would be fatal.

Even with all the opportunities for improvisation, the arranger is far more important to a swing band than the conductor, the players, or the composers who supply the tunes. Many arrangements are made for a particular band and never published at all, possibly not even written out completely. The general effects are laid out by a genius whose name the public may never hear at all. Certain choruses are always left to the improvisation of inspired soloists, although even here there may be a suggestion of basic figures for the decoration of the melody. A complete arrangement is generally worked out in rehearsal, retaining the effects that prove their value and discarding those that do not. With the arranger as a guide, and with frequent suggestions from individuals in the band, the final version may be the result of endless experimentation, perhaps never actually arriving at a fixed permanence of any kind.

ARRANGEMENTS SPELL SUCCESS

Successful swing bands guard their own arrangements jealously, for it is upon them that their individual reputation depends, even though the leader may get all the credit. Outstanding swing-leaders are generally soloists of the spectacular type and deserve their success from the standpoint of performance rather than conducting. They also rank high as personalities, executives and business men, and some of them manage to achieve a reputation on the strength of these qualities alone.

It must be remembered that swing is merely a form of jazz, often duplicating the type called "hot jazz," and that jazz itself is not a *kind* of music, but a *way of playing* which can be applied to practically any material.

[207]

Jazz treats popular music in exactly the same way, fundamentally, as modernism applies to serious composition. Both may be called briefly "the distortion of the conventional," and this distortion is by no means limited to the treatment of rhythm.

Syncopation, sometimes called "ragtime," is the most familiar form of musical distortion, and many people think that this is the entire essence of jazz. But syncopation distorts only the rhythmic factor in music, anticipating or delaying the natural beat so as to cause artificial accents.

DISTORTIONS OF MELODY

While syncopation definitely affects the melody as well as the rhythm of a composition, the commonest melodic distortions are of the conventional form known as "variations," and this is carried to its ultimate extreme in the "breaks" and "hot licks" of swing. Both syncopation of rhythm and variations on melodies are common in the classics of music, and the specialists of swing are, therefore, merely giving a new twist to long-standing commonplaces of composition.

Distortions of harmony and tone color also are nothing new. Composers have experimented with harmony and discord from the time that Monteverde first used a deliberate dissonance for dramatic effect, about the end of the sixteenth century. Beethoven, Chopin, Wagner, Debussy, Scriabine, and Schoenberg all made important innovations in harmony, completely revising the accepted rules of the musical text-books. Experimentation with instrumental quality, generally known as "tone color," has been equally common, with Berlioz among the pioneers and Stravinsky an outstanding modern representative.

All these distortions enter significantly into the modern form of popular music called, for no particular reason, "swing." (It should not be assumed that all swing is fast and loud and "hot.") Effects of syncopation, far beyond those of the old-fashioned "ragtime," the decoration, elaboration, and often complete concealment of melodies through improvised or set variations, the use of acrid, often discordant harmonies and of exaggerated tone colors, secured through the muting of brass, slapping of string basses, unusually high registers of clarinets and trumpets, and insistently spectacular percussion (including not only drums, but xylophone, vibraphone, piano, and guitar as well)—these are the common and necessary characteristics of swing. It is only in their application by individual players and arrangers that originality and novelty are attained.

Actually the raucous, haphazard jazz-players of over twenty years ago were doing exactly the same thing in a cruder style. They did not have the skill of today's performers, or the highly developed instruments for self-expression. But they made use of the same basic distortions, in a fairly obvious and generally noisy fashion, and their jazz had all the fundamental qualities of real folk-music. For even in its primitive manifestations, folk-music invariably depends upon monotony of rhythm, simplicity of melody, exaggerated tone color, and the spirit of improvisation, and these all enter into the modern effects of jazz and swing. It is entirely fair to call this modern popular music the only real folk-music of America, showing all the fundamental characteristics of the primitive type, but in a highly sophisticated form, and largely based upon the true folk-music of the Negro, which, however, we have no right to claim as our own, any more than we can claim that of the Indian, the Oriental, the Jew, or the primitive English, Scotch, or Irish creator of ballads, from which most of our mountain and cowboy music is borrowed.

SWING HAS ITS MERITS

In spite of this perfectly logical ancestry, there can be no question of the distinctive originality of swing. It is a development of old and well-tried tendencies, closely allied to the idiosyncrasies of human nature in general, but it has resulted in something that is highly individual and thoroughly American, whether you like it or not. Its most successful interpreters are those who apply the principles of syncopation and decorative improvisation most skillfully and individually, with an unerring instinct for the maintenance of a fundamental rhythm and melodic line, even amid the wildest distortions imaginable. The secret of effective swing is that rare gift of keeping just off the beat and playing all around the melody without ever losing track of the fundamental structures involved.

There are two different styles of swing, one of which might be called the African and the other the Dixieland or New Orleans school. The first is characterized by even and heavy accents on all four beats of each measure, suggesting the effect of an actual African drum or tom-tom. The Dixieland, or New Orleans, type of swing emphasizes artificial accents on the second and fourth beats (the "off beats") and generally concentrates more upon syncopation than on a steady rhythm. Practically all swing music can be placed in one of these two classes, and while the first is probably the more popular, the second has greater possibilities for finesse.

With new bands constantly springing up and new leaders, soloists, and arrangers acclaimed overnight, it is impossible to single out all the interpreters and creators of swing that are worthy of mention, nor can any attempt be made at a grading or classification that would hold good for any length of time. Some of the best exponents of swing may still be working quietly and obscurely, known perhaps to the specialists and to their own colleagues, but destined never to achieve the lime-light of publicity. There are a few names, however, which the layman should know, even though he may seldom read them in the papers.

Perhaps the most important of these names is that of Fletcher Henderson, who is just beginning to receive proper credit for the variety, originality, and beauty of his swing arrangements. Henderson is a Negro pianist who has had a band of his own, but who started merely as an arranger of a rather different type. He made all of the earlier arrangements for Benny Goodman, and it was his work that made up practically the entire program at Carnegie Hall, when swing gave its first concert demonstration. Recently Fletcher Henderson has made arrangements for Tommy Dorsey, and he has also had a number of "stock arrangements" published, which all bands are able to use. He may be considered the most musical of the swing arrangers, and certainly an excellent model for the lesser lights.*

THESE ARRANGERS ARE SIGNIFICANT

Less known to the public, but perhaps equally important, is Jim Mundy—a colored trumpeter, originally with the Earl Hines band—who followed Henderson as arranger for Benny Goodman and for a time worked exclusively for that virtuoso of the clarinet. When Gene Krupa, the spectacular drummer, left Goodman to form his own band, Mundy went with him as arranger. His work is of the "killer-diller" type, full of intense excitement and enormously appealing to the jitterbugs.

Quiet, unassuming, and scholarly, a young Negro named Edgar Sampson has come forward as one of the most significant of the swing arrangers. He plays the alto

* Since this paragraph was written, Henderson has returned to the Goodman fold and is now the band's regular pianist.

saxophone and has been a member of the Ellington, Henderson, and other bands. The keynote of his work is simplicity. He does not believe in asking the players to strain for their effects, and he has solved the problem of making swing-music sound exciting and elaborate without actually making great demands on the skill of the performers. Sampson is a close student of the theory of music and intends to work for a doctor's degree in his chosen subject.

The most complicated swing arrangements are probably those of Don Redman, Negro sax and clarinet player, who also leads his own band, with earlier experience at the head of McKinney's Cotton Pickers, one of the greatest of all jazz groups of the past. Redman's name is held in veneration by most swing-players and arrangers, black or white.

Among colored arrangers the name of Duke Ellington, brilliant pianist, conductor, and composer, still stands high, but he is today a creator rather than an arranger of music. He has real significance as an inventor of musical effects and a pioneer of swing, and is an outstanding example of the type of musician that can produce a complete and elaborate piece of swing directly in rehearsal, without writing down a note of music. (Ellington actually did this in preparing a short motion picture for which a piece was to be specially "composed.")

Benny Carter's name should also be mentioned among the Negroes of swing. He plays trumpet and saxophone and now has his own band to lead. His arrangements are of the Henderson type, with emphasis on beauty and musicianship.

Of the white boys, one of the youngest and greatest stars is Bob Haggart, string bass player in Bob Crosby's band and chief arranger for that organization. His colleagues consider Haggart the best bass player in the country, and he also plays the trumpet, guitar, and piano. His arrangements are in the true Dixieland style, although he was born in Douglaston, Long Island.

Matty Matlock, who plays clarinet in the same band, is also a skilled arranger of the Dixieland school, formerly with Ben Pollack in one of the most famous of swing combinations. This original New Orleans group also included Crosby's great drummer, Ray Bauduc; Eddie Miller, king of the hot tenor sax; Gil Rodin, another tenor saxophonist; and the Crosby guitarist, Nappy Lamare.

Organizer of the bands of the Dorsey brothers and Ray Noble, and arranger for them as well, is Glenn Miller, a white trombonist who commands the respect of all swing-musicians. He now has his own band and continues to make arrangements of all-round effectiveness, "sweet and hot." He is responsible for such innovations as increasing the saxophone section from four to five instruments, with an added clarinet.

Eddie Sauter, originally arranger for Red Norvo, and more recently associated with Benny Goodman's outfit, is an average trumpeter but a brilliant and original artist when it comes to swing treatment, with an unusual feeling for harmony and tone color. He is never satisfied with his work, which may be one reason why it possesses such consistent distinction.

Of the old-time arrangers (which means those of only a few years ago) Jimmy Dale, Archie Bleyer, Frank Skinner and others are still important. Another good man today is Spud Murphy, who has his own band, and there is Ben Pollack's original arranger, Dean Kincaide, who also worked for Bob Crosby and now devotes his talents to the cause of Tommy Dorsey.

Will Hudson, who wrote the *Organgrinder's Swing* and other successful songs, was a partner of Eddie DeLange and arranged the music for the band known by their names. Hudson eventually took over this band and, after recovering from a nervous breakdown, has now started his own band again. (Why don't more swingsters have that experience?) Commercially Hudson has been most successful, although not an instrumentalist in the strict sense.

YOU KNOW HIS SONGS

Another commercial success, on an even larger scale, has been that of Larry Clinton, who climbed to sudden fame and fortune by making popular songs out of Debussy's *Rêverie* (*My Revery*) and Tschaikowsky's *Romeo and Juliet* (*Our Love*). His swing arrangements are conventional but practical, employing mostly the well established type of "blue" strain. His original numbers include the sensational *Dipsy Doodle* and *Satan Takes a Holiday*.

In the older swing-bands three saxophones and three brasses (two trumpets and a trombone) were considered sufficient, but today one finds at least four saxophones (two tenor and two alto, all doubling as clarinets) and five additional brass instruments (three trumpets and two trombones), with the conventional rhythm section of piano, drums, string bass, and guitar. Violinists are scarce in modern swing-bands except for an occasional "hot fiddler" like Joe Venuti, who leads his own outfit.

Outstanding pianists of the swing school are Count Basie, whose methods are deceptively quiet and unobtrusive, Teddy Wilson, starring in Benny Goodman's quartet, "Fats" Waller, perhaps the dean of them all, Jess Stacy, Joe Sullivan, and Bob Zurke.

MASTERS OF THE LICORICE STICK

Clarinet honors are a toss-up among the one and only Benny Goodman, Artie Shaw, and Bob Crosby's "Fazola," whose real name is Irving Prestopnick. Jack Teagarden remains the king of the hot trombonists, now leading his own band, and by many of the experts he is considered the best jazz musician of all time. That title is disputed by the Negro Louis Armstrong, trumpeter extraordinary and hoarse-voiced singer in a manner all his own, and definitely also by Goodman and the legendary Bix Beiderbecke (hero of the book, *Young Man with a Horn*), whose records prove him to have been a most musical and sensitive player of the trumpet.

Goodman, Shaw, Crosby and the Dorseys all maintain their high standing as white swing-leaders, with Harry James, Glenn Miller, Gene Krupa, Bunny Berigan and a few others claiming recognition. Jimmie Lunceford stands high as a swing specialist among the colored leaders, with Duke Ellington, Count Basie, and Cab Calloway all holding their own, the last named perhaps inclined to bury his band in a circus of individual showmanship.

Something should be said also about the six-piece colored band at the Onyx Club, led by John Kirby, which gets remarkable results from the simple combination of alto sax, clarinet, trumpet, string bass, piano, and drums. Among the white musicians, Raymond Scott has done clever things with his quintet, although his work appeals to the intellect rather than the emotions.

A DICTIONARY OF COMMON SWING TERMS*

(*Mostly in the artificial vocabulary of the jitterbugs*)

Ad lib: To improvise.
Alligator: A follower of swing.
Ballied: Ballyhooed, publicized.

* These definitions are based upon the following books in the rapidly growing literature of jazz and swing: *American Jazz Music*, Wilder Hobson (W. W. Norton & Co.); *Jazz—Hot and Hybrid*, Winthrop Sargeant (Arrow Editions); *Hot Jazz*, Hugues Panassie (M. Witmark & Sons); *The Kingdom of Swing*, Benny Goodman (Stackpole Sons); *Love in Swingtime*, Tommy Dorsey and George D. Lottman (Exclusive Publications); *Yearbook of Swing*, P. E. Miller (Down Beat Publishing Co.).

[217]

Barrelhouse: Free and easy, relaxed.
Blackstick: Clarinet.
Blip: Excellent.
Boilers: Large drums.
Book man: A good reader of music.
Break: Impromptu phrase, interrupting the melody.
Breakdown: To perform original variations.
Busteroo: Failure. (Cf. *Flopperoo.*)
Canary: A female vocalist.
Cats: Hot musicians.
Clambake: A jam session, *q.v.*
Click: Succeed.
Corny: Mediocre, old-fashioned, rural.
Cut: Make a record.
Dillinger: Something very hot.
Dixieland: The New Orleans style of swing.
Dog house: Bass fiddle.
Flopperoo: Failure, complete flop.
Formats: Arrangements.
Front man: Band leader.
Get-off man: Soloist.
Gitbox: Guitar.
Gobstick: Clarinet.
Go to town: Get very hot.
Groanbox: Accordion. (Also *Squeezebox.*)
Guthucket: Hot jazz at its best.
Hides: Drums.
Hot jazz: The opposite of sweet jazz.
Icky: Ignorant, an ignoramus.

[218]

In the groove: Perfect.

Jam session: Swing played for the performers' own amusement.

Jitterbug: Swing fanatic.

Jive: To talk the swing lingo.

Killer diller: Swing with a terrific thrill.

Kopasetic: All right, O.K.

Lick: An improvised hot phrase.

Licorice stick: Clarinet.

Long hair: Classical musician.

Long-underwear guy: The same as above.

Low down: Blue, torchy, sad.

Madhouse: Headquarters of the Musicians' Union.

Name band: A band having a leader of reputation.

Nitery: Night club.

Paper men: Readers, not improvisers.

Platter: Phonograph record.

Powerhouse: The rhythm section.

Push pipe: Slide trombone.

Plumber: Trumpeter.

Razzmataz: Pre-war popular music.

Scat singer: One who sings nonsense rhythmically.

Schmaltz: Sentimental music.

Screwball: Any swing-musician.

Send: To arouse the emotions.

Skins: Drums.

Squeakbox: Violin.

Straight: Legitimate, conventional.

Sugar band: A sweet-playing band.

Suitcase: The drums.
Sweet: Smooth, not hot.
Swing: Improvised variations on popular tunes.
Turkey: A failure.
Woodpile: Xylophone.
Wah-wah: Sound of a muted trumpet.

AMERICA'S MUSICAL PROBLEM

When the New York World's Fair first announced its musical program, it was disappointingly noticeable that American composers and interpreters had been practically ignored. It was, in effect, an admission to the world that the United States had no musicians of its own worthy of being presented on such an occasion.

Actually, this is far from the truth, but it expresses a traditional inferiority complex that has for years retarded the development of our native music. Perhaps the obvious success of our popular music has served to emphasize this lack of confidence in our more serious musical efforts. Our jazz and swing have been the envy of the whole world, and our Broadway revues and musical comedies have set a standard that no other country has recently equaled.

Tin-Pan Alley grinds out popular hits with monotonous regularity, and the commercial returns of such American music are definite. Meanwhile, the men who would like to write symphonies and other serious

[221]

compositions are mostly either starving to death or working at something else to make a living.

The absurd attitude of the World's Fair was immediately challenged by a newly formed National Committee for American Music, which commanded attention if only because it represented all the important musical organizations of the country. Its polite but firm reminders of the existence of a significant literature of serious American music were given apparently sincere consideration by Grover Whalen and his Chairman of Music, Olin Downes, and it was only the complete collapse of the Fair's musical program that prevented at least a belated recognition of the American composer. The United States government should have subsidized a festival of American music, just as the foreign governments paid for advertising their art.

THE HONEST JITTERBUG

Meanwhile, our serious music-lovers, whether honest or not in their protestations, could well take a lesson from the devotees as well as the promoters of jazz and swing. Such a thing as an inferiority complex never enters the heads of these practical people. The jitterbugs know that they are getting a kick out of the music, and that is all that matters. They do not stop to analyze their feelings or to ask questions or make apologies; nor do the publishers and players of popular music. To them it either makes money or it does not. If it is commercially successful, it must be good. Otherwise it is not worth bothering about.

The basis of all this is confidence and a lack of self-consciousness. Popular music lives upon the same human reactions as does folk-music itself. These reactions are fundamentally honest, even though they may be stimulated nowadays by clever devices of merchandising and propaganda. But even the best of popular hits can be "plugged" only so far. Sooner or later it must stand on its own feet and trust to the inherent reality of its appeal. In practically every case its life is limited, for such music does not usually possess any of the qualities of permanence. It is of the "easy come, easy go" type, quick in its success and equally or even more quick in its decline.

Nobody ever had to be trained to respond to folk-music or its urban counterpart. It either registered or it did not, and there was little or no talk of educating the listener to its appreciation or understanding.

But "serious" or "classical" music has always labored under the handicaps of uplift and intellectual improvement. People have been told that they ought to like Bach, Beethoven, Brahms, and Wagner, and it has sometimes been difficult for even such great composers to overcome that psychology.

MISPLACED ENTHUSIASM

Similarly, American music has been presented as a duty, perhaps with emphasis on patriotism rather than musical values. It has been further handicapped by the

[223]

indiscriminate zeal of those who unhesitatingly bally-hooed anything as long as it was American. Naturally when so much of this material proved itself obviously weak and unfit to compete with the solid music of the world, a permanent prejudice was created in the minds of those who really had some taste and judgment in such matters.

Even today there are far too many amateurs asking for recognition as composers and vociferously proclaimed by their friends, with the result that one hears an over-abundance of absurdly inadequate compositions and not nearly enough of the things that deserve and would reward serious attention. This brings up the real problem of American music, which is that no discriminating audience, capable of honest and authoritative appraisal of unfamiliar works, has yet been developed in this country.

Such an audience is unquestionably in the making. Radio and the phonograph have helped to make a great new public appreciative of the things that have already proved their permanence. More recently the Federal Music Project has unearthed a huge number of people who never before could afford to listen to good music at first hand and who now are discovering it with the most sincere and natural reactions imaginable. Out of such audience response a practical appraisal of American music may yet result.

The trouble with our established concert and operatic audiences is that they were built upon formulas, traditions, catchwords, and hypocrisies. They were not only unwilling but unable to express an honest opinion that had any value whatever. They depended on the newspaper critics, who profited by the glamour of the printed word, and on the neighbors who could bandy the technical terms most convincingly.

WHEN DOCTORS DISAGREE

Even well-educated musicians and music-lovers are notoriously untrustworthy in their reactions to the art. It is almost impossible for them to rid themselves of prejudices and petty personalities and jealousies. Consult a half dozen of them on any really debatable musical question, and you will get completely varying opinions. Boiled down, it all amounts to the fact that each self-appointed critic is contemptuous of any other opinion and merely sure of his own absolute infallibility, no matter how vague and purely personal his reactions may be. His refuge is generally a withering scorn that effectively silences any timid commentator who might have a significant idea of his own. It is only when you compare notes that you find critics of the same standing equally scornful of exactly opposite opinions, with no real confidence in themselves and certainly no justification for their omniscient attitude.

Unfortunately, a great many good musicians are stupid, unreasonable, selfish, and intolerant. In fact, intolerance is the besetting sin of all those who deal in music as its creators, interpreters, propagandists, or

[225]

appreciators. It has held back music in general for years, and it is holding back American music to-day.

The worst offenders are the extreme modernists, to whom everything of the conventional type, including even some well-established classics, is old-fashioned and reactionary. By insisting on whole programs of sustained cacophony, unrelieved by anything simply melodious or potentially popular, they set up a barrier between themselves and the audience whose good will they need so desperately. Between the extremists and the deluded amateurs, America's creative music has its own difficulties in making a favorable impression at home.

FOREIGN METHODS AND INFLUENCES

But there is a possible middle ground, and it has been sufficiently proved that American composers, if given a chance, can more than hold their own with any of the foreigners today. What they lack is not musical knowledge or significant materials, but a command of the technique of musical politics and intrigue. In that respect, as compared with our European competitors, we are still babes.

Servility to foreign standards became a habit with Americans at a time when our own music was actually limited and mostly an imitation of what was accepted abroad. We were taught music by foreigners, who naturally used the materials of their own musical education, so that an endless chain was gradually forged, with no place for any American links. We were led to believe that no good music could come out of this country, except perhaps some folk-like tunes of the Foster type.

The visiting foreigners who continued to make an excellent living out of American dollars assiduously preserved this legend. They habitually played, sang, and conducted European works, mostly of unquestioned value and fairly obvious appeal. When they introduced novelties at all, it was in a spirit of chauvinism, and even the greatest artists have not been entirely free from that tendency.

THE EUROPEAN SYSTEM

Abroad, any visiting artists are automatically compelled to perform the music of the country that is extending its hospitality to them, but here the situation is exactly reversed. As great a genius as Toscanini himself has stooped to the performance of mediocre Italian music for presumably national and patriotic reasons (and, of course, making it sound important by his unparalleled art) while consistently ignoring American music, or, at the most, making an occasional unconvincing gesture in its direction.

At one time the prejudice against American musicians in their own country was so great that native artists not only had to make their reputations abroad but actually had to change their names so as to give them a foreign sound, before presenting themselves to audiences of their fellow-citizens. Foreign study was considered absolutely essential to a musical career, and foreign debuts and criticisms, most of which could be bought for a definite price, were valued beyond all reason or common sense.

For a nation of practical business executives, we have shown a strangely unpractical attitude toward the arts and particularly toward music. We have permitted typically European intrigue to take advantage of our ignorance, and while we have given our greatest financial rewards to artists whose ability was unquestioned, we have often paid undeserved tribute to mediocrities and occasionally have been deceived by downright charlatans.

The fault again lies in our willingness to substitute an artificial snobbery for honest and intelligent appraisal of musical values, and this fault has its inception in the traditional tendency to consider music a duty or a fad instead of a normal and totally unpretentious pleasure. It is still an open question whether the insincere follower of "the classics" deserves a higher rating in the scale of civilization than the blatantly honest fanatic of jazz. If the two could be rolled into one, with an equal distribution of sincerity and knowledge, you would have a real music-lover.

WORTH-WHILE AMERICAN COMPOSERS

While America's most effective music is still in the popular field, with some utterly charming works of permanent appeal by such gifted composers as George Gershwin, Jerome Kern, Richard Rodgers, Arthur

Schwartz, and Cole Porter, our serious creative work has also by this time established both its immediate effectiveness and its permanent value. Our musical pioneers, such as MacDowell, Chadwick, Parker, Converse, Hadley, and Stillman-Kelley, are worth playing indefinitely, and they continue to supply the staples of most American programs.

But to these solid musicians of the older school have been added numerous composers of the transitional type, among whom the names of John Alden Carpenter, Howard Hanson, Arthur Shepherd, Deems Taylor, Leo Sowerby, David Guion, John Powell, Daniel Gregory Mason, Charles T. Griffes, Ernest Schelling, W. G. Still, and R. N. Dett are outstanding. There are also men who belong somewhere between the serious and popular classifications, like Ferde Grofé, Vernon Duke, and Robert Russell Bennett.

Perhaps the most important of the American composers of solid attainments, sufficiently modernized, is Harold Morris, whose concertos and a recent symphony, *Prospice*, place him on a high plane, judged by any standards. A comparative newcomer, Paul Creston, twice elected to a Guggenheim Fellowship, shows equal promise. Aaron Copland is better known than either of these, and is more inclined toward modernism, but his talents justify his position and he has amply proved his ability to write good music of all kinds.*

* Copland has also shown that he can write interestingly and instructively about music in his recent book, *What to Listen For in Music* (Whittlesey House).

Randall Thompson, Douglas Moore, Samuel Barber, Virgil Thomson (who wrote the music for Gertrude Stein's *Four Saints in Three Acts* and the motion picture, *The River*), Abram Chasins, Emerson Whithorne, Quincy Porter, Harl McDonald, Roy Harris, Philip James, Charles Haubiel, Eric Delamarter, and others are contributing significantly to American music, with varying degrees of seriousness and popularity represented by Gail Kubik, Louis Edgar Johns, Charles Sanford Skilton, Horace Johnson, A. Walter Kramer, Charles Wakefield Cadman, Bainbridge Crist, Anton Bilotti, Samuel Barlow, Wintter Watts, Otto Luening, Mortimer Browning, Elliot Griffis, Mabel Daniels, M. Wood-Hill, Lily Strickland, Arthur Farwell, Henry Holden Huss, Frederick Jacobi, Howard Murphy, and others.

Walter Piston, Roger Sessions, and Marion Bauer are fairly consistent in their modernism, with George Antheil, Henry Cowell, Carl Ruggles, and Charles Ives perhaps representing a still more radical tendency, and such younger men as William Schuman, Marc Blitzstein, Elie Siegmeister, Harrison Kerr, Paul Nordoff, Robert McBride, Gardner Read, and David Diamond varying in their devotion to older and newer schools of musical thought. If one includes naturalized as well as native Americans in the list, then we can today claim such giants as Schoenberg, Rachmaninoff and Ernest Bloch, along with other important Europeans who are now American citizens, and our past musical history would thus include figures like Charles Martin Loeffler on the serious side and Victor Herbert in the more popular field. Regardless of where the line is drawn, the materials of American music are now almost unlimited. They are merely waiting to be discovered by the American public.

If our composers can become a little more practical, a little more tolerant, perhaps a little more patient, and if they will occasionally condescend to write music that everyone would like, playable by average amateurs as well as professionals, we can look forward to the universal recognition of American music in all its forms. We may not produce much more in the way of symphonies, operas, or chamber music, for these conventional types would seem to have had their possibilities fairly well exhausted in the past and to fit rather clumsily and artificially into the modern tempo. America's music of the future is likely to make some use of the idioms of jazz, just as all European music utilized the folk-strains of its individual countries. It is likely to be a practical, utilitarian music, expressed chiefly through such thoroughly modern agencies as the screen, radio, television, and instruments that can produce, by electrical amplification and control of tone color, effects that had never before been heard. Hints of such music have already been given, and everything points toward the development of American music along these lines.

SOME PRACTICAL COOPERATION

Meanwhile, various organizations are working sincerely and efficiently in behalf of America's musical artists. The National Committee for American Music has already been mentioned. The National Music Council may some day make the United States government aware of the importance of our native art, which has thus far been officially ignored except for the relief measures of the Works Progress Administration.

The National Association for American Composers and Conductors, founded by the late Henry Hadley, is exceedingly active in arranging for performances of serious music, including broadcasts, and is gradually assembling a complete reference library of American music in the larger forms, to be housed in a special room at the headquarters of New York's Public Library, at Forty-second Street and Fifth Avenue. A lending library of classic scores is available for the use of orchestral conductors, on condition that they include American works in all programs utilizing this material.

Publication of American music is stimulated by this organization, as well as by the Henry Hadley Foundation, the Juilliard Foundation, and such non-profit-making groups as the Society for the Publication of American Music, the Composers Press, and the Arrow Music Press. The recording of American compositions is also receiving attention, with the big commercial companies beginning to recognize its possibilities after courageous pioneering by the society known as New Quarterly Recordings.

The National Federation of Music Clubs emphasizes its policy of supporting the American composer and interpreter, and the National Bureau for the Advancement of Music, which organizes and regularly manages National Music Week, promotes the same idea in its program. The Federal Music Project has consistently presented American music throughout the country, and in recognition of this service its former director, Nikolai Sokoloff, was recently awarded the Henry Hadley medal, with a certificate of merit also to Ashley Pettis for his direction of the Composers Forum-Laboratory, a unique institution which brings together the composer and his audience for immediate discussions of American music and reciprocal reactions.

OTHER AMERICAN ORGANIZATIONS

There is an American Composers Alliance, chiefly concerned with performing rights, and an American Guild of Musical Artists, which amounts to a union of the performers in the concert and opera fields. The American Guild of Organists encourages native composers, as do the National Music Educators, the League of Composers (recently active in launching the American Lyric Theater), the American Choral and Festival Alliance, the Intercollegiate Music Guild of America, the American Composers Committee, the Society of Professional Musicians, the Music Teachers National Association, the Alumni Association of the Juilliard Graduate School, the National Association of Schools of Music, the Music Library Association, and the leading musical fraternities and sororities.

Most practical of them all is the American Society of Composers, Authors and Publishers. While primarily concerned with the collection of royalties for the public performance of commercially valuable music, as a clearing-house between the creators of such material and the entertainment interests that use it for profit, ASCAP today solves the problems of many a serious musician by subsidizing him, in effect, paying for the prestige of his name with money largely earned by the popular songs of his fellow-members. The society thus achieves a distinction and musical significance far beyond its obvious importance as a business organization.

CONCLUDING OPTIMISTICALLY

So the cause of American music is by no means hopeless. There are enough people working for it earnestly and effectively to offset the vast amount of silly talk that has been wasted on the subject, and perhaps to overcome eventually the prejudices, mechanical formulas and false complexes that have proved so destructive in the past. A big step forward will have been taken when the 99 per cent of America's potential music-lovers have arrived at an honest enjoyment of what has always been at their disposal, perhaps even supplanting the sacred 1 per cent of the elect who have so often frightened them away. Such an ideal is by no means impossible for those who have learned literally to take their music for fun.

THE PROOF OF THE PUDDING

You may think that this book has been merely theorizing, but that is not the case at all. Every one of the suggestions made here has been carried out, not once but many times.

There *are* parents in America who have given music to their children from the very start, and some of them are already making music-teachers happy. Every musical prodigy that you hear about—in fact, every mature musician of prominence—started in just that way. If a decided talent had not shown itself by the age of six or seven, a career was practically out of the question. Germany produced the world's greatest composers in rapid succession, not because of some inborn gift for music, but because in practically every German home it was taken for granted that everybody could and should make music. Out of such universal participation, individual geniuses were bound to emerge.

There are musical families in America today, but not enough of them, chiefly because there is not enough home life in general. When people do stay at home, the radio and the phonograph make music too easy, and participation is not encouraged, although there are programs and records with which ambitious amateurs may play along, and there is always the fun of acting as private conductor to a real orchestra.

HE-MEN WHO ENJOY MUSIC

Before closing this argument in favor of music for fun, it may be worth while to cite specific instances of important and successful Americans who are getting fun out of music and have been doing so for years. There are so many of them that one is almost tempted to claim that music and practical success go hand in hand.

Take a look at a few statesmen, politicians, and business leaders, for instance. President Roosevelt loves to hear old songs and relaxes best when he listens to such music played by a piano-accordion. Former Governor Al Smith, of New York, also leans toward the old ballads and can sing them in a husky but effective bass. He likes nothing better than an old-fashioned barbershop quartet. His son-in-law, Major Warner, is an accomplished pianist, who plays concertos and jazz equally well.

Mayor La Guardia, of New York, the son of an Italian bandmaster, is a sincere music-lover, and hears the Philharmonic Orchestra and the Metropolitan Opera as regularly as possible. He surprised radio listeners by his excellent comments on a symphonic program over the air not long ago and actually conducted the Philharmonic at the opening concert of the New York World's Fair.

The late Nicholas Longworth, son-in-law of Theodore Roosevelt, was a first-class violinist and regularly gave informal concerts of chamber music at his Washington home. Charles M. Schwab, the steel magnate, has a pipe organ in his New York house and plays on it for his own pleasure, besides engaging the professional organist, Archer Gibson, for private concerts. Cyrus H. K. Curtis, publisher of the *Saturday Evening Post*, was also an excellent organist, and George Eastman, of kodak fame, not only endowed the Eastman School of Music in Rochester but held informal concerts regularly in his home.

MUSIC AGREES WITH BUSINESS

Another business-man organist, who is likewise a composer, is Dr. Herbert Tily, head of the Strawbridge and Clothier store in Philadelphia and for many years conductor of its big chorus. It was a surprise to find several years ago that Cyrus H. McCormick, of the International Harvester Company, had composed and privately published a number of songs and piano pieces. His interest in music was very deep, and to the end of his life he regretted that he had not been allowed to devote more time to it. His brother Harold is an opera fan and an expert whistler.

The late Edward T. Stotesbury, of Philadelphia, a world famous financier, loved to play the drums, and always gave himself a special treat of drumming on his birthday. Adolph Lewisohn's specialty was singing, which he did with great enthusiasm even after he had reached his middle eighties. He was particularly fond of *The Two Grenadiers*.

MOVIE STARS LIKE MUSIC

The motion pictures are full of good musicians and sincere music-lovers. Charlie Chaplin plays the violin really well and composed all the music for his picture, *Modern Times*, a remarkably effective score. Marlene Dietrich is also a good violinist and plays the piano besides. Robert Taylor thought seriously of becoming a professional cellist and went to Pomona College for that purpose. Jimmy Cagney can play his own piano accompaniments for cowboy songs and gets a lot of fun out of it. The musical accomplishments of the Marx Brothers are, of course, well known, although Groucho does not often show his skill on the guitar.

Ernst Lubitsch plays Viennese waltzes like the native that he is, and a number of other directors and stars can do their bit at the piano. Dick Powell plays several instruments excellently, and so does Fred MacMurray.

Fredric March and his wife, Florence Eldridge, are both music-lovers, listening constantly to good records at home. Both are now taking singing-lessons, and Mrs. March and the children also work at the piano together. Their friend Kay Johnson, wife of the director,

John Cromwell, is a fine pianist, but plays entirely for her own pleasure.

The stage has two excellent pianists in Ethel Barrymore and Otto Kruger. Neysa McMein, the artist, also plays well, and novelist Fannie Hurst is good enough to play duets with her professional pianist husband, Jacques Danielson.

"Uncle Dan" Frohman, dean of the theater, is one of the prize exhibits of *Music for Fun*. In his late eighties he could still play snatches of a number of pieces on the piano, to his great satisfaction. He never bothered to learn an entire composition, but picked up as much as he could "by ear," and then went on to something else. In this way he was constantly stimulating his musical memory, which was prodigious.

MUSIC AND RELATIVITY

The mathematician, Albert Einstein, a self-taught amateur violinist, is another important figure that will be remembered as one who had fun with music. Playing sonatas at sight has always been his chief relaxation from scientific labors.

Among the writers, John Erskine comes close to professional standards as a pianist, but this might be expected of the former president of the Juilliard School of Music. Vicki Baum, who wrote *Grand Hotel*, is primarily a harpist, but also plays the piano. Hendrik Willem van Loon is a rough-and-ready violinist who gets a lot of fun out of playing informally, and successfully edits a song-book from time to time. The late Montague Glass could play almost anything on the piano by ear, and he knew a choice lot of musical stories.

Franklin P. Adams (F.P.A.) gets fun out of a harmonica, a xylophone, or a concertina. His wife, a granddaughter of the song-writer, George Root, plays the piano well, and two of their boys are working at the clarinet and the trumpet. Victoria Lincoln (*February Hill*) is also a harmonica player, and perhaps the star of the harmonicamateurs is the painter, Thomas Hart Benton, who has taught his wife and little boy to do their part in making up a family trio.

Among the athletes there is plenty of music for fun. Philadelphia Jack O'Brien, once a world's champion boxer, still plays the violin, with perhaps just a touch of the *Golden Boy* complex. Mickey Cochrane, of the Detroit Tigers, has been a good enough saxophonist to appear in vaudeville, and Charlie Grimm, of the Chicago Cubs, has the reputation of being an excellent banjo player. "Pepper" Martin, of St. Louis, organized his own band, the "Mudcats," which enlivened many a ball game; and of course there is a vocal quartet in practically every baseball or football squad.

Big Bill Tilden, former world's tennis champion, has one of the best collections of phonograph records in America and is a serious music-lover. Don Budge and his former doubles partner, Gene Mako, are of the jitterbug type, but they also carried a phonograph with them, as Tilden used to. Mako would like to be a trap drummer, and loves nothing better than to sit in with a professional band and try all the tricks.

Before this book ends, two musical families should be mentioned. One is the Simon family of New York, and the other is the Drinker family of Philadelphia.

Richard Simon, who heads the publishing firm of Simon & Schuster, is the eldest of four brothers, all of whom get fun out of music. Richard himself plays the piano better than he likes to admit, but shares this recreation with tennis and bridge. His brother Henry (whose wife wrote the best seller, *With Malice toward Some*) is also a good tennis and bridge player but specializes in the violin. The third brother, Alfred, first learned the piano, but picked up the accordion in order to get a part in a play which demanded that accomplishment. George, the youngest, spent his boyhood as a trap drummer, accompanying phonograph records, with baseball and tennis on the side. He paid his way through Harvard with his music and is now writing a column on swingbands for the musical magazine, *Metronome*, of which he has recently been made editor-in-chief. A cousin, Robert Simon, is music critic of *The New Yorker*, and his wife is a professional pianist, Madeleine Marshall. The Simon family has had no reason to regret the time spent on music.

The father of the Drinkers was President of Lehigh University, and the famous artist, Cecilia Beaux, was an aunt. They were not particularly musical, but developed the habit of playing and singing together as children. Today Harry Drinker, a prominent Philadelphia lawyer, lives next door to his sister, Mrs. Catherine Drinker Bowen, who wrote *Friends and Fiddlers* and the book about Tschaikowsky, *Beloved Friend*. She is an amateur violinist and he a composer, conductor, and pianist. Both have trained their children musically so that they can at any time assemble a string quartet or larger instrumental combination and produce some really good music. This is without any help of heritage or tradition. Mr. Drinker has written a scholarly booklet on the chamber music of Brahms and contributed significant articles to various musical journals. On Sunday evenings he often invites a group of musical amateurs to his home to sing Brahms or Bach or Palestrina at sight or to play instrumental ensembles. That, of course, represents an ideal that is bound to be increasingly rare nowadays, for those who have the ability do not as a rule have the time or the inclination to play together in such informal fashion.

MORE MODEST IDEALS

But even if home music falls far short of the Drinker or the Simon standards, it can be fun for those concerned, and if it is only started early enough in a growing family, there is no telling how far it may develop. The main object of this book is to encourage that early start. If it is already too late for that, then start anyway, getting some fun out of music in some way, and don't worry if you don't seem to get very far. The greatest mistake is to feel that music is worth while only if one reaches the heights. That simply is not true. Any sincere response to music of any kind has its significance, for it represents a human reaction that may eventually become the common ground of great art and great artists.

The grim determination to like the good things merely because one has been told that they are good spells practically no progress in the potential music-lover's development. The hypocritical pretense that conceals an inferiority complex is even worse.

We can afford to be honest with ourselves, even if we do not seem to be going ahead very fast. If we take our music as we would any other recreation, trying to take some active part in it, trying to arrive at some intelligent appreciation of a truly great performance or composition, but never losing sight of the importance of our personal and sincere enjoyment, Music for Fun becomes not only a practical possibility, but something infinitely to be preferred to the lugubrious, reverential, awe-struck ceremonies that have come to be so widely considered a sacred duty. You are the only one who knows whether you are honestly enjoying music or not. Let no one deprive you of that privilege.

APPENDIX

On the following pages will be found a chronological chart showing the years of the birth and the death of every composer who could fairly be called important, plus the birth-dates of a few living composers whose significance is universally recognized. No living Americans have been included among the latter, for obvious reasons of diplomacy, as well as an honest uncertainty as to their future positions. A number of them unquestionably deserve a place in the list, and their names will be found in the chapter on American music.

A chart like this has never before been attempted in such detail, and it is hoped that the small type will be excused in view of the necessity of getting many names and dates into a limited space. The reader who has the patience to follow out a number of the date-lines will be rewarded with some interesting facts. He will be reminded forcibly of the short span of life enjoyed by a Mozart, a Schubert, a Mendelssohn, or a Gershwin. He will note the enormous chronological advantage of a Verdi over a Wagner, born in the same year. He may occasionally be surprised to find that certain composers were contemporaries, whose lives he had never considered parallel in time.

At least this chart should have some value for quick reference, when questions of musical chronology come up, as they do so frequently in these days of intensive self-education and the cheerful dissemination of knowledge.

[244]

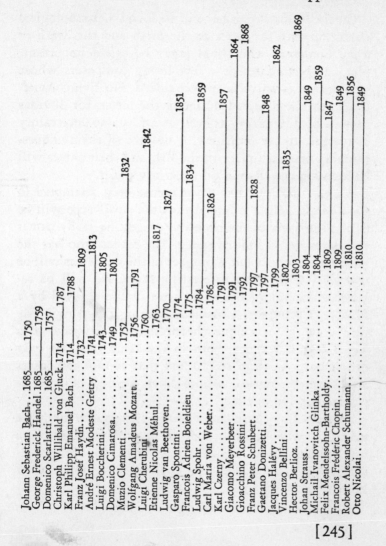

Johann Sebastian Bach	1685	1750
George Frederick Handel	1685	1759
Domenico Scarlatti	1685	1757
Christoph Willibald von Gluck	1714	1787
Karl Philipp Emanuel Bach	1714	1788
Franz Josef Haydn	1732	1809
André Ernest Modeste Grétry	1741	1813
Luigi Boccherini	1743	1805
Domenico Cimarosa	1749	1801
Muzio Clementi	1752	1832
Wolfgang Amadeus Mozart	1756	1791
Luigi Cherubini	1760	1842
Etienne Nicolas Méhul	1763	1817
Ludwig van Beethoven	1770	1827
Gasparo Spontini	1774	1851
Francois Adrien Boieldieu	1775	1834
Ludwig Spohr	1784	1859
Carl Maria von Weber	1786	1826
Karl Czerny	1791	1857
Giacomo Meyerbeer	1791	1864
Gioacchino Rossini	1792	1868
Franz Peter Schubert	1797	1828
Gaetano Donizetti	1797	1848
Jacques Halévy	1799	1862
Vincenzo Bellini	1802	1835
Hector Berlioz	1803	1869
Johan Strauss	1804	1849
Michail Ivanovitch Glinka	1804	1859
Felix Mendelssohn-Bartholdy	1809	1847
Francois Frédéric Chopin	1809	1849
Robert Alexander Schumann	1810	1856
Otto Nicolai	1810	1849

Franz Liszt...1811 ———— 1886
Richard Wagner.1813 ———— 1883
Giuseppe Verdi..1813 ———— 1892
Robert Franz....1815 ———— 1890
Niels Gade......1817 ———— 1893
Charles Francois Gounod.1818 ———— 1893
Jacques Offenbach......1819 ———— 1880
César Franck...........1822 ———— 1890
Anton Bruckner.........1824 ———— 1896
Friedrich Smetana......1824 ———— 1884
Johann Strauss, Jr.....1825 ———— 1899
Stephen Foster.........1826 ———— 1864
Karl Goldmark..........1830 ———— 1915
Anton Rubinstein.......1830 ———— 1894
Johann Svendsen........1832 ———— 1888
Johannes Brahms........1833 ———— 1897
Alexander Borodin......1834 ———— 1887
César Cui..............1835 ———— 1918
Camille Saint-Saens....1835 ———— 1921
Léo Delibes............1836 ———— 1891
Alexandre Guilmant.....1837 ———— 1911
Mily Balakirew.........1837 ———— 1910
Georges Bizet..........1838 ———— 1875
Max Bruch..............1838 ———— 1920
Modeste Moussorgsky....1839 ———— 1881
Peter Iljitch Tschaikowsky..1840 ———— 1893
John Stainer...........1840 ———— 1901
Anton Dvorak...........1841 ———— 1904
Emmanuel Chabrier......1841 ———— 1893
Arrigo Boito...........1842 ———— 1918
Jules Massenet.........1842 ———— 1912
Arthur Sullivan........1842 ———— 1900
Nikolai Rimsky-Korsakoff..1844 ———— 1908

Gabriel Fauré, 1845 — 1924
Vincent d'Indy......1851 — 1931
Charles Villiers Stanford..1852 — 1924
Engelbert Humperdinck...1854 — 1921
G. Whitfield Chadwick...1854 — 1931
Edward Elgar.........1857 — 1934
Giacomo Puccini......1858 — 1924
Victor Herbert.......1859 — 1924
Ignace J. Paderewski...1859
Gustav Mahler........1860 — 1911
Hugo Wolf............1860 — 1902
Edward A. MacDowell...1861 — 1908
Isaac Albeniz........1861 — 1909
Claude Debussy.......1862 — 1918
Ethelbert Nevin......1862 — 1901
Frederick Delius.....1863 — 1932
Horatio Parker.......1863 — 1919
Pietro Mascagni......1863
Richard Strauss......1864
Jean Sibelius........1865
Gustave Charpentier..1869
Henry K. Hadley......1871 — 1937
Alexander Scriabine..1872 — 1915
Max Reger............1873 — 1916
Sergei Rachmaninoff..1873
Arnold Schoenberg....1874
Maurice Ravel........1875 — 1937
Ottorino Respighi....1879
Ernst Bloch..........1880
Igor Stravinsky......1882
Sergei Prokofieff....1891
George Gershwin......1898 — 1937

Index